Jerry D. Wilson
Lander College

Instructor's Resource Manual for
PHYSICS LABORATORY EXPERIMENTS
Second Edition

D.C. HEATH AND COMPANY
Lexington, Massachusetts   Toronto

Published simultaneously in Canada.

Printed in the United States of America.

International Standard Book Number: 0-669-09910-4

PREFACE

This Instructor's Resource Manual that accompanies the second edition of <u>Physics Laboratory Experiments</u> is supplied at the request and suggestion of several instructors who used the first edition of the laboratory manual. It provides several resources that most of us have wished to have at hand at one time or another.

Some instructors wish to test students on laboratory experiment principles. To assist with this Post-Lab Quiz, Questions (with answers) are provided for each experiment. Also, comments and hints on laboratory experiments and procedures are given. These come from personal experiment and input from various physics instructors, in particular, Professor I. L. Fisher of Bergen Community College, Paramus, New Jersey. In addition, Answers to Selected Experiment Questions are given for your convenience.

You will also find references for laboratory safety manuals, a list of scientific equipment suppliers, and a summary of major equipment needs for planning purposes. The equipment summary indicates which pieces of equipment may be used in different experiments for maximum utilization.

Finally, graph copy masters are included so that you may inexpensively supply students with common graph paper if you wish. It is hoped that you will find this Resource Manual helpful. Should you think of other items that might prove helpful in laboratory instruction, suggestions are welcomed.

Jerry D. Wilson
Lander College
Greenwood, SC 29646

CONTENTS

Experiment 1   EXPERIMENTAL ERROR AND DATA ANALYSIS

Comments and Hints

    This experiment is considered to be an important initial
operation for students. It is inexpensive and the principles
learned will be applied in error and data analyses in following
experiments.

(a)   Because the sets of data taken in most experiments
have only several values and do not lend themselves to
statistical analyses, the section in this experiment on
standard deviation is labeled as optional. As the instructor,
it is your option to include this section. It is considered
to be instructive for students to be at least introduced
to such concepts. On the other hand, the time of the laboratory
period and student speed may be a limiting factor.

(b)   Of particular importance is the section on Graphical
Representation of Data. It has been the experience of the
author that students generally submit poor graphical repre-
sentations of data (i.e., they turn in lousy graphs). This
is in the form of graphs with unlabeled axes and omission
of units, straight lines connecting data points (Fig. 1-
6, Graph A) instead of smooth curves, etc. It is strongly
recommended that major emphasis be placed on proper graphing
procedures. It is highly important that persons in science
fields know how to graphically represent data properly.

    A concept introduced here and used in various experiments
is the reduction of nonlinear functions to linear functions
of the form y = ax + b so they may be plotted on Cartesian
coordinates and the slope and intercept values determined.
This should be stressed. (The graphing of exponential functions
on semilog and log-log graph paper is the subject of Experiment
52.)

(c)   Optional equipment in this experiment are students'
hand calculators (for ease of calculations) and French curves.
The latter may be shown as a demonstration or used by the
students in drawing curves if you have a sufficient quantity
available.

1

Completion

1. Errors associated with measurement instruments or techniques are called __systematic errors__.

2. Errors resulting from unknown and unpredictable variables in experimental situations are called __random errors__.

3. In general, the accuracy of an experimental value depends on __systematic errors__ and the precision on __random errors__.

4. If there is no decimal point in a number, the __rightmost nonzero__ digit is the least significant figure.

5. To avoid problems with zeros in significant figures, __powers-of-ten or scientific notation__ may be used.

6. To express percent error, an __accepted__ value must be known.

7. The average value of a set of measurements is sometimes called the __mean__ value.

8. In the equation of a straight line, y = ax + b, the a is the __slope__ of the line and b is the __y-intercept__.

9. The slope of a straight line on a graph is the ratio of __$\Delta y/\Delta x$__.

10. For a straight line on a graph (y = ax + b), the x-intercept (y = 0) is given by __-b/a__.

Multiple Choice

1. The type of error which is associated with measurement instruments or techniques is (a) personal error, *(b) systematic error, (c) random error, (d) mathematical error.

2. The type of error that is minimized by making a large number of measurements and taking the mean value is (a) personal error, (b) systematic error, *(c) random error, (d) mathematical error.

3. The type of error on which the precision of a measurement generally depends is (a) personal error, (b) systematic error, *(c) random error, (d) incorrect significant figures in calculations.

4. The correctness of an experimental measurement is expressed in terms of (a) significant figures, *(b) accuracy, (c) precision, (d) personal error.

5. The comparison of two equally reliable experimental measurements is often expressed in terms of *(a) percent difference, (b) percent error, (c) average or mean value, (d) significant figures.

6. The average or mean value of an experimental set of data gives the best value when the measurements involve only (a) personal error, (b) percent difference, (c) significant figures, *(d) random error.

7. The y-axis of a Cartesian graph is called the (a) mean, (b) abscissa, *(c) ordinate, (d) slope.

8. The plotting of two variables such as T <u>versus</u> θ generally means that the θ values are plotted on the *(a) x-axis, (b) ordinate axis, (c) slope, (d) y-axis.

9. Error bars on a graph give an indication of (a) units, (b) abscissa values, (c) accuracy, *(d) precision.

10. The slope of a straight line graph is given by the (a) x-intercept, (b) y-intercept, *(c) ratio of a particular ordinate difference and the corresponding abscissa difference, (d) ratio of the maximum x-axis scale to the y-axis scale.

Essay

1. Distinguish and explain the difference between straight-line graphs with positive slopes and negative slopes.

2. What would cause a "skew" or shift of the maximum of a normal or Gaussian distribution of experimental values?

Experiment 2 MASS, VOLUME, AND DENSITY

Comments and Hints

To introduce students to experimental measurements, length and mass measurements are made in this experiment and the densities of various materials computed. The concept of instrument scale least count is introduced, which further reinforces significant figures (or digits) in measurements, in particular, the estimated or doubtful figure. Density computations give practice using significant figures in calculations. Students are also introduced to the vernier caliper and micrometer, which are usually unfamiliar measurement instruments.

General student difficulties in this experiment arise from:

(a) reading a vernier scale. Should you wish to emphasize the convenience of the metric system, try having them use the upper English vernier scale, but most wisely after the students have learned the use of the lower metric scale.

(b) The double rotation of the micrometer thimble for a 0.01 mm spindle movement. The idea of a double "50 cent" rotation to give "one dollar" as described in the experiment has been found to be helpful.

Answers to Selected Experiment Questions

3. Use a sinker weight attached to the floating object by means of a string to immerse the object. Note the cylinder reading with only the sinker immersed, then the cylinder reading with both the sinker and object immersed (cf. Experiment 25).

4. Given: r = 20 cm, t = 0.50 mm = 0.050 cm, ρ_{Al} = 2.7 g/cm^3 (Appendix Table A1).

$$V = At = (\pi r^2)t = \pi(20)^2(0.050) = 63 \text{ cm}^3$$

$$m = \rho V = (2.7)(63) = 170 \text{ g} = 1.7 \times 10^2 \text{ g}$$

Note: students understanding the experiment seem to have little problem with Archimedes' problem in Question 5.

4

Exp. 2
POST-LAB QUIZ QUESTIONS

Completion

1. If an instrument scale has a least count of 1 cm, it
   can be read to the nearest __0.1 cm or millimeter__ .

2. A vernier scale is useful in reading the fractional
   part of the __least count__ .

3. A negative zero correction is __added__ to measurement
   readings.

4. When two rotations are required to move a micrometer
   thimble through 1.0 mm, the pitch of the micrometer
   screw is __0.5 mm__ .

5. The instrument most convenient for measuring the inner
   diameter of a ring would be the __vernier caliper__ .

6. The rachet mechanism on a micrometer permits the jaw to
   be tightened on objects with the same __force__ .

7. Density provides a measure of the __compactness__ of
   matter in a substance.

8. The units of density are __kg/m^3 or g/cm^3__ .

9. If two different size objects have the same mass, the larger
   object has a __smaller__ density.

10. In terms of density, the mass of an object is given
    by __$m = \rho V$ (density times volume)__ .

Multiple Choice

1. The instrument in the experiment with the smallest least
   count was the (a) meter stick, (b) vernier caliper,
   *(c) micrometer, (d) all were the same.

2. The diameter of a round pencil or pen is most conveniently
   measured with a (a) meter stick, *(b) vernier caliper,
   (c) micrometer, (d) graduated cylinder.

3. Before making a measurement, it is always important
   to check the instrument's (a) mass, (b) least count,
   (c) length, *(d) zero correction.

5

4. The function of a vernier scale is to (a) increase the least count, *(b) assist in accurately reading the fractional part of a scale division, (c) allow inner diameters to be easily read, (d) avoid positive zero corrections.

5. The main scale of a micrometer is on the (a) anvil, (b) spindle, *(c) sleeve, (d) thimble.

6. If a micrometer screw had a pitch of 1.0 mm and there were 50 divisions on the thimble, then a thimble division corresponds to (a) 0.01 mm, *(b) 0.02 mm, (c) 0.05 mm, (d) 0.10 mm.

7. A piece of dust or foreign matter on the flat jaw surface of the anvil of a micrometer could give rise to a (a) more accurate reading. *(b) positive zero correction, (c) negative zero correction, (d) random error.

8. If object A had twice the mass and one-half the volume of object B, then the density of A would be *(a) four times that of B, (b) twice that of B, (c) the same as that of B, (d) one-half that of B.

9. A graduated cylinder has a linear <u>length</u> scale on its side calibrated in volume units because (a) it is a vernier scale, (b) length and volume are the same, *(c) the cross-sectional area of the cylinder is assumed to be uniform, (d) it allows for different liquid densities.

10. An average density is obtained when (a) an object is irregularly shaped, (b) significant figures are not used in calculations, (c) personal error is involved, *(d) the object substance is not pure or homogenous.

Essay

1. Discuss the use of a balance on the moon. Would it accurately determine mass?

2. Could a meter stick be equipped with a vernier scale? If so, design one. (Illustrate with a sketch.)

3. Explain how the linear scale on a graduated cylinder is calibrated in volume units. How would scales vary with different size cylinders?

Experiment 3 MEASURING THE HEIGHT OF A BUILDING

Comments and Hints

   This is a fun experiment, particularly on a nice fall day when students are chomping at the bit to get outside (and often request to hold the laboratory outside). However, it can be a valuable learning experience, mainly for classes in which the fundamentals of trigonometry have just been introduced. This simple experiment allows students to apply trigonometric principles and ingenuity.

   Given only (a) two meter sticks and/or (b) one meter stick and a protractor, students are asked to design their own experimental procedures in measuring the heights of a couple tall objects on campus.

   (a) With two meter sticks, the sides (hypotenuse and side adjacent) of a similar triangle can be measured and the interior angle found. With this angle and the distance from the tall object to the observation point, the height of an object can be determined using tan θ (see comment below).

   (Some students may use similar triangle ratios to find the height instead of trigonometric functions. You may wish to restrict them to trigonometry methods, however, they are usually pleased to have thought of the similar triangle method. The trigonometric solution may be given later as an exercise.)

   (b) With a meter stick and protractor, the angle may be measured directly and the height of the object found. A string and weight help in accurately reading the angle.

Comment: In both methods, it is convenient for the students to stand erect in making measurements. You may wish to tell them this. (They tend to try to make measurements on the ground and may get a bit dirty.) Of course, the sighting height must be added to the computed object height if the base length is taken from the object to the observation point in this case. Students tend to forget this and it makes for good post-exercise discussion and analysis to promote student learning.

   Although a simple experiment, it gives the instructor a variety of options. It is suggested that different lab teams make measurements by different equipment methods and give reports on their experimental procedures when returning to the lab. You may instructively point out sources of experimental error at this time. As suggested in the experiment, an optional error analysis may be done on the team results to find the class average and compared to the actual object heights if known.

Experiment 4   THE SCIENTIFIC METHOD: THE SIMPLE PENDULUM

Comments and Hints

The simple pendulum is a standard introductory physics lab experiment.   In this presentation, effort is made to couple the experimental procedure with the scientific method approach to investigations.   Also, the idea of a "black box" system is introduced to emphasize the concept of system parameters in experimental investigation.

A "free" lab variation of this experiment is to simply ask students to physically describe a pendulum system without being given any theoretical background.   This is a challenging approach, but fails to incorporate the scientific method in checking theoretical predictions against experimental results.

One noted common student error in the experimental procedure is to have the plane of the pendulum oscillation perpendicular to the axis of the pendulum clamp (or parallel to the clamp screw) such that the string hits the clamp bar below the point of suspension during oscillations.   A commercially-available pendulum clamp is recommended for ease of adjusting pendulum lengths.

Answers to Selected Experiment Questions

2.   With T = 1 s,

$$L = gT^2/4\pi^2 = (9.8)(1)^2/4\pi^2 = 0.25 \text{ m (2 significant figures)}$$

3.   (a) $\theta = 10°$, L = 1 m

$$T_1 = 2\pi(L/g)^{\frac{1}{2}} = 2\pi(1/9.8)^{\frac{1}{2}} = 2.0 \text{ s}$$

$$T_2 = 2\pi(L/g)^{\frac{1}{2}}(1 + \tfrac{1}{4}\sin^2\theta/2) = 2.0 (1 + \tfrac{1}{4}\sin^2 5°) = 2.0 \text{ s}$$

percent difference = 0 (2 significant figures)

Exp. 4

(b) $\theta = 60^\circ$, $L = 1$ m

$$T_1 = 2\pi(L/g)^{\frac{1}{2}} = 2.0 \text{ s} \quad \text{as in (a)}$$

$$T_2 = 2\pi(L/g)^{\frac{1}{2}}(1 + \tfrac{1}{4}\sin^2\theta/2) = 2.0\,(1 + \tfrac{1}{4}\sin^2 30^\circ) = 2.1 \text{ s}$$

$$\text{percent difference} = \frac{T_2 - T_1}{(T_2 + T_1)/2} \,(\times\ 100\%)$$

$$= \frac{2.1 - 2.0}{(2.1 + 2.0)/2}\,(\times\ 100\%) = 4.9\%$$

POST-LAB QUIZ QUESTIONS

Completion

1. Testing theoretical predictions against experimental results is the principle of the __scientific method.__

2. The length of a pendulum is measured from the point of suspension to the __center (of mass) of the bob__.

3. The theoretical expression $T = 2\pi(L/g)^{\frac{1}{2}}$ is a __first-order__ approximation.

4. The theoretical expression $T = 2\pi(L/g)^{\frac{1}{2}}\,[1 + \tfrac{1}{4}\sin^2\theta/2]$ is a __second-order__ approximation.

5. A "black box" relationship connects the __input and output__ parameters of a system.

6. In a "black box" representation, the measured quantities are called __output__ parameters.

7. The period of a simple pendulum is dependent on the pendulum __length__ and __angle (of oscillation)__.

8. The period of a simple pendulum is independent of the __mass of the bob__.

9. In a Cartesian plot of L versus T of the first-order approximation for a simple pendulum, the curve is a __parabola.__

9

10. If L versus T^2 is plotted on a Cartesian graph for the first-order approximation for a simple pendulum, the graph is a __straight line__ with $g/4\pi^2$ as __its slope__.

Multiple Choice

1. Testing theoretical predictions against experimental results is called (a) first-order approximation, (b) second-order approximation, (c) trial-and-error, *(d) scientific method.

2. The length of a simple pendulum is determined by the (a) angle of oscillation, (b) mass of the bob, *(c) center (of mass) of the bob, (d) friction of the support.

3. When the length and mass of the bob of a simple pendulum are increased, for small angle oscillations, *(a) the pendulum swings more slowly, (b) the first-order approximation is no longer valid, (c) the general theoretical period no longer depends on θ, (d) the scientific method is no longer applicable.

4. In a black box representation, the output parameters (a) are independent variables, (b) are independent of all of the independent variables, *(c) describe the behavior of the system, (d) are absent in a simple pendulum system.

5. When the angle of oscillation of a simple pendulum exceeds the first-order approximation, the period (a) depends on the mass of the bob, (b) is uneffected, (c) is less than the first-order approximation, *(d) increases.

Essay

1. Describe how a simple pendulum might be used to experimentally determine g (the acceleration due to gravity).

2. Discuss the black box representation and effects with T, m, and θ as input parameters.

3. The third term in the theoretical series expansion for the period of a simple pendulum is $+(9/64)\sin^4\theta/2$. Show what contribution this would make to the first-order approximation of the period for an angle of 30° ($\sin 30^\circ = 0.50$).

Experiment 5 UNIFORMLY ACCELERATED MOTION

Three methods of investigating uniformly accelerated motion are presented: A. Object in Free Fall, B. Free-Fall Spark-Timer Apparatus, and C. Linear Air Track. Obviously, the timing of dropped object in A is the simplest, but perhaps the least instructive because of the lack of intermediate measurements. Even so, it makes a good introduction to the more complicated B and C methods.

Comments and Hints

A. Object in Free Fall

The method is straight forward. A reaction time correction is made to call student attention to this timing consideration. (See Experiment Question 3 below.)

B. Free-Fall Spark-Timer Apparatus

Since high voltages are involved, detailed instructions in the use of the spark-timer should be given if the students make the data tapes. Some instructors prefer to prepare a number of tapes for student use before hand and show how this is done as a demonstration at the beginning of the lab period. (This also reduces equipment requirements.)

Helpful hints in experimental procedure and data analysis, as provided by Professor I.L. Fischer, Bergen Community College, are as follows:

Experimental Procedure

(a) Before making electrical connections, tighten the front and rear wires on the drop tower. Clean the wires (#22 steel wire) rubbing lightly with sandpaper or steel wool. For best results, the wires should be kept taut and clean.

(b) Make certain the apparatus is properly connected. A 6 VDC power supply is connected through a switch to the electromagnet at the top of the drop tower. The spark generator is connected to the drop tower's vertical wires at the bottom of the tower. The <u>high voltage</u> connection on the generator is terminal at the end of a long insulator, which may be labeled "danger -- high voltage". The lead from this terminal should be attached to the <u>front</u> wire of the tower via <u>high voltage insulated</u> electrical wire. The low voltage lead from the generator (labeled "ground" or "gnd") attaches to the rear wire and body of the tower via common insulated electrical wire.

CAUTION: Do not touch the high voltage lead or the front wire on the tower while the spark generator is on (even if sparks aren't produced).

(c) Adjust the drop tower to be vertical. Temporarily remove the paper tape so that the front and rear wires are both visible. Switch on the electromagnet and suspend a long plumb bob from it. Adjust the feet of the tower so that the plumb bob hangs evenly between the wires. Check bob centering from front to back and side to side. For best results, use the longest possible plumb bob.

(d) Make a tape and check to see if it is evenly and completely marked. If not, further adjustments may be needed. Do not waste tape. If a tape is poorly marked, use the same tape repeatedly while making adjustments. Only for the "final" run should a fresh tape be utilized.

A tape is useable even if it is missing one or two spots, provided the missing spots may be isolated and the time scale can be established without ambiguity. A graph can be prepared from such a tape by simply omitting the missing data points.

Data Analysis

(e) Use a vernier caliper to measure the first few values of y_i up to about 12 cm. Use a meter stick for the larger values of y_i. Remember that the measured distances are the <u>total</u> distances from the reference line, and <u>not</u> the distances between adjacent lines. (Use of the vernier caliper allows more significant figures for the first few measurements and greater accuracy.)

(f) When graphing, mark the abscissa (x-axis) in units of spark-timer intervals, e.g., 1/60 s, rather than normal time units. This choice of scale factor makes it much easier to plot the data.

C.   Linear Air Track

There are a variety of air tracks available, as well as timing gates and accessories. The instructor may have to modify specific experimental procedures somewhat to apply to a particular air track. Also, if electronic timing gates are used, which provide better accuracy, students will require instruction on the use of these sensitive apparatuses.

Exp. 5
Answers to Selected Experiment Questions

A.   Object in Free Fall

3(a).   An estimate of a person's reaction time may be made
by dropping a ruler or meter stick through the person's
curled hand and measuring the stick length that falls through
the hand before it is grasped.   Suppose on the average the
stick descends 15 cm or 0.15 m before it is grasped.   Then, with
$y = 0.15$ m, $v_o = 0$, and $g = 9.8$ m/s^2, using $y = \frac{1}{2}gt^2$,

$$t = (2y/g)^{\frac{1}{2}} = \left[\frac{2(0.15)}{(9.8)}\right]^{\frac{1}{2}} = 0.17 \text{ s}$$

B.   Spark-Timer Apparatus

4.   From eq. 5-6, $v_1 + v_o = 2y_1/t_1$.   Using Eq. 5-4 to determine
   the value of v_1 (with $\bar{v} = v_1$),

$$v_1 = (y_2 - y_o)/(t_2 - t_o) = y_2/t_2$$

where $y_o = t_o = 0$.   Substituting into Eq. 5-6,

$$v_o = 2y_1/t_1 - y_2/t_2$$

Remark: v_1 as computed above is an <u>average</u> velocity.   However,
since the acceleration is constant, <u>the average velocity for the</u>
time interval $t_2 - t_o$ is the <u>instantaneous</u> velocity v_1 at t_1,
the middle point of the time interval.

POST-LAB QUIZ QUESTIONS

Completion

A.   Object in Free Fall

1.   If air resistance were taken into account for a falling
     object, the measured acceleration would be <u>less</u>   than
     g.

13

2. If the falling object were given an initial downward velocity, the actual value of g would be __unaffected__, but using $y = \frac{1}{2}gt^2$ to compute g with the measured experimental data, the computed value would be __greater__ than g.

3. Not taking into account the reaction time correction would give rise to a __systematic__ error that would give an experimental value __greater__ than g.

B. Spark-Timer Apparatus

4. For a uniformly accelerated object, the average velocity over a time interval is equal to the __instantaneous velocity__ of the object at the middle of the time interval.

5. The instantaneous velocities computed in the experiment, $v_i = 2y_i/t_i$, are not the actual velocities of the object because it had __an initial velocity__ at the designated t_o.

6. If the designated t_o spot on the data tape had actually been the initial time of release ($t = 0$), then the plot of v_i versus t would have an intercept at __the origin__.

C. Linear Air Track

7. When one end of the air track is elevated, the glider moves down the track under the influence of a __component__ of g.

8. The greater the elevation of the end of an air track, the __less__ its travel time to the opposite lower end.

9. The maximum acceleration of the glider released from rest is achieved for an elevation angle of __90^o__, in which case, the acceleration is __g__.

Multiple Choice

A. Object in Free Fall

1. For a freely falling object on the moon, which of the following equations would apply? ($g = 9.8$ m/s^2)

   (a) $y = v_o t/6 + \frac{1}{2}gt^2$, (b) $y = \frac{1}{2}gt^2$, (c) $y = v_o t + \frac{1}{2}gt^2$,

   *(d) $y = v_o t + gt^2/12$

14

2. A dropped object traveling a long distance on earth is not in free-fall with an acceleration of g because of (a) initial velocity, (b) a zero final velocity, *(c) air resistance, (d) personal error.

3. If an object in free-fall were dropped through one-half of a previously dropped distance, (a) its acceleration would vary, *(b) the instantaneous velocities would be the same during the falls, (c) $y = \frac{1}{2}gt^2$ would not apply, (d) the acceleration for the shorter distance would be g/2.

B. Spark-Timer Apparatus

4. In computing the acceleration of the falling object, it is necessary to *(a) know the spark-timer interval, (b) not have any missing spots, (c) know the voltage of the spark-timer, (d) know the total length of the tape.

5. If a second data tape were made with a spark-timer frequency of 30 Hz instead of 60 Hz, on the second tape the (a) acceleration would be different, (b) the spots would be closer together, *(c) the computed instantaneous velocities would be greater for corresponding numbered spots, (d) the spots would be separated by twice the distance.

6. The x-intercept on the v versus t graph of the data corresponds to *(a) $t_o = 0$ at time of release, (b) $\bar{v}$, (c) initial acceleration, (d) a random error.

C. Linear Air Track

7. If the air flow to the air track were reduced for some reason, this would result in *(a) a systematic error, (b) a greater experimental acceleration, (c) a shorter glider distance for an elevated track, (d) a smaller percent error.

8. For a greater elevation height h of an air track, the sin θ (a) decreases, *(b) increases, (c) remains the same, (d) has a smaller angle θ .

Experiment 6   THE ADDITION AND RESOLUTION OF VECTORS:
               THE FORCE TABLE

Comments and Hints

This experiment helps enforce the methods of vector
addition, in particular, the graphical method. It may be
the only time students have a "forced" introduction to graphing
vectors, which heightens their appreciation for the relatively
quick and convenient analytical methods -- particularly
the component method. Some common student difficulties
encountered are:

(a) Problems with graphing "to scale". It has been
found to be instructive to talk about the familiar
example of drawing a house floor plan to scale with
a scale factor of ft/in. This may be compared to N/cm
for a vector scale factor.

(b) The law of cosines is used in initial analytical
methods. Students tend to forget how to use this law.
A pre-lab review is helpful.

(c) A few students have trouble with distinguishing
between the force table equilibrant and the vector
resultant, and why the resultant cannot be found directly
on a force table.

Answers to Selected Experiment Questions

3.   Using a free-body diagram with the nail at the origin
     and T = 3.5 N at θ = 45°,

     (a) The sum of the upward (y-direction) tension forces is
     equal to the upward reaction force of the nail:

$$R = 2T_y = 2T\sin 45^{o} = 2(3.5)(0.707) = 4.9 \text{ N}$$

     (b) The upward reaction force equals the weight of
     the picture (static equilibrium), and

$$w = R = 4.9 \text{ N}$$

You may wish to ask the students what the weight of
the picture is in the customary unit of pounds as a
mental conversion exercise. With 1 kg being equivalent
to 2.2 lb and F = mg = (1 kg)(9.8 m/s^2) = 9.8 N, the
conversion factor of 2.2 lb/9.8 N is deduced, and

$$w = 4.9 \text{ N } (2.2 \text{ lb/9.8 N}) = 1.1 \text{ lb}$$

Exp. 6

4. As in 3 above, using a free-body diagram with the origin at the foot pulley,

(a) for the horizontal reaction force R_x,

$$\sum F_x = 0 = T\cos 60^\circ + T\cos 30^\circ - R_x$$

and

$$R_x = T\cos 60^\circ + T\cos 30^\circ = (50)(0.50) + (50)(0.866) = 68 \text{ lb}$$

(b) Looking at the y-components of the cord tensions,

$$T\sin 60^\circ - T\sin 30^\circ = (50)(0.866) - (50)(0.50) = 18 \text{ lb}$$

which is the net vertical force exerted on the foot. This is balanced by the downward reaction force of the foot (partial weight) and R_y = 18 lb.

POST-LAB QUIZ QUESTIONS

Completion

1. A vector quantity has magnitude and direction .

2. Two vectors may have the same magnitude but be different because of different directions .

3. The polygon method is really an extension of the triangle method.

4. The scaling factor of the graphical method of vector addition represents the ratio or conversion factor of vector magnitude to the graph vector length .

5. When there is a 90° angle in a triangle, the law of cosines may be reduced to the Pythagorean theorem .

6. Any vector may be resolved into rectangular components .

7. In terms of x and y rectangular components, the magnitude of a vector is given by $F = (F_x^2 + F_y^2)^{\frac{1}{2}}$ and the direction by $\theta = \tan^{-1}(F_y/F_x)$.

8. The vector -A has the same magnitude as a vector A, but is opposite in direction .

9. On a force table, the resultant of a set of vectors is equal in magnitude to the equilibrant, but __opposite in direction__ .

10. A force table angle of 240° corresponds to an angle relative to the negative x-axis and quadrant of __60°, third quadrant__ .

Multiple Choice

1. A vector differs from a scalar in that a vector has (a) units, (b) magnitude, *(c) direction, (d) a symbol.

2. The sum of two or more vectors is called (a) a component, (b) a negative vector, (c) the Pythagorean theorem, *(d) the resultant.

3. The addition of two vectors not at right angles by the analytical triangle method requires the use of *(a) the law of cosines, (b) the Pythagorean theorem, (c) $\tan \theta = B/A$, (d) resolution of components.

4. When vectors are added by the graphical method, the vectors are (a) resolved into components, *(b) plotted to scale, (c) subtracted, (d) without a resultant.

5. In the analytical component method of vector addition, the orientation (direction) of the resultant as given by $\theta = \tan^{-1} (F_y/F_x)$ is relative to the (a) origin, (b) one of the vectors, *(c) x-axis, (d) y-axis.

6. When force vectors in newtons are plotted to scale using a centimeter scale, the scaling factor has units of (a) N/cm^2, (b) N-cm, (c) cm/N, *(d) N/cm.

7. The equilibrant determined on a force table is (a) the same as the resultant, (b) 90° to the resultant, *(c) opposite in direction to the resultant, (d) twice the magnitude of the resultant.

Essay

1. Are there any vector additions that cannot be represented on a force table? Explain.

Experiment 7 NEWTON'S SECOND LAW: THE ATWOOD MACHINE

Comments and Hints

This experiment has been refined in the second edition so students may obtain better experimental accuracy. In addition to a correction for friction (m_f), a correction for the pulley's rotational inertia is made (m_{eq}). It is important to note that these corrections are used in the <u>theoretical</u> expression and calculations. That is, the ideal <u>theoretical</u> expression is modified so as to better describe the experimental results. Friction and inertia are inherent in the experimental apparatus and will be included automatically in the experimental results.

The following helpful comments on these points were contributed chiefly by Professor I. L. Fischer, Bergen Community College.

Concerning the equivalent mass of the pulley (m_{eq}):

Unfortunately, there are no massless pulleys. Omitting the moment of inertia of the pulley can cause quite large errors when $m_1 + m_2$ is small. Adding m_{eq} to the $m_1 + m_2$ term in Eq. 7-4 helps reduce this source of error.

For a uniform disk, the value of m_{eq} is taken as half the mass of the pulley*. However, some pulleys are not removable from their brackets, so the mass of the pulley cannot be measured; and in any case, pulleys are not usually uniform disks.

A rather quick way of "measuring" m_{eq} is to experimentally measure the acceleration a_m as in Experiment Procedures 2-4. Use minimum $m_1 + m_2$ to accentuate the effect of m_{eq} over m_f. (See comments on friction below.) Determine m_f as in procedure 3 and compute m_{eq} from Eq. 7-4(a).

Concerning friction in the Atwood machine:

Friction in the Atwood machine occurs at the pulley hub, and at the rim of the pulley where the cord changes curvature. The friction at both these places increases

---

*$\tau = I\alpha$, and $m_2 gR - m_1 gR = (MR^2/2)(a/R) = MRa/2$, which reduces to $m_2 g - m_1 g = (M/2)a$.

with cord tension, which in turn depends on the total suspended mass. Therefore, the force of friction may be considered constant only so long as the total suspended mass remains constant. Whenever the total mass is changed, as in the constant force-varying total mass portion of the experiment, friction should be remeasured before each trial as indicated.

A further complication arises because the pulley hub friction is somewhat velocity dependent. Consequently, even the most careful measurement of m_f may be in error because the constant velocity during the m_f measurement procedure is not the same as the "average velocity" during the acceleration trial.

Suggestions:

(a)   Lubricate the pulley hub with a lubricant such as WD-40. This should reduce the overall friction, and hopefully, the variation of friction with velocity.

(b)   Make the friction measurements with the masses moving at reasonably high speeds, which simulates the actual conditions during the acceleration trials. Measuring friction when the masses are barely moving gives a false high value for m_f.

(c)   Use a thin cord or string looped over the largest pulley of a multiple pulley set for minimum friction. Beware of stretching if thin nylon cord is used. The stretching becomes pronounced when the total weight is increased, and is observable even with a constant weight as time goes on. For any type cord, it is a good practice to have students measure y for every acceleration trial due to stretching, even in the constant mass portion of the experiment.

(d)   If your budget can withstand the strain, use ball-bearing pulleys especially designed for this experiment. If not, multiple pulley sets have the advantage of a large pulley so that the ascending and descending masses do not come into contact as they pass each other.

Answers to Selected Experiment Questions

1. Yes.   In Newton's second law, $F = ma$, the mass m is the _total_ mass of the moving system. Since the string has mass and is in motion, its mass should be included. Note: how this is done is beyond the scope of an introductory physics course. The string contributions to m_1 and m_2 involve a dm/dt calculus solution. Most students

answer this question incorrectly because of a misunderstanding of the term "negligible" (mass). The purpose of the question is to point out that for extreme accuracy no contribution is totally "negligible" and the meaning of Newton's law as described above.

3. Eq. 7-4a,

$$a = (m_2 - m_1 - m_f)g/m$$

$$= (g/m)(m_2 - m_1) - m_f g/m, \text{ where } m = m_1 + m_2 + m_{eq}$$

and $y = ax + b$.

4. Eq. 7-4a as above,

$$1/a = (m_1 + m_2 + m_{eq})/(m_2 - m_1 - m_f)g$$

$$= [1/(m_2 - m_1 - m_f)g] (m_1 + m_2) + m_{eq}/(m_2 - m_1 - m_f)g$$

and $y = a x + b$.

POST-LAB QUIZ QUESTIONS

Completion:

1. In $F = ma$, the force F is a(n) __unbalanced or net__ force.

2. The pulley in the Atwood machine simply acts as a __direction changer__.

3. The equivalent mass term m_{eq} corrects for __(rotational) inertia__.

4. When the mass system of an Atwood machine moves with a constant velocity, the net force is __zero__.

5. If the theoretical formula for acceleration were not corrected for friction, the predicted value would be too __large__.

6. The acceleration of a system varies __inversely__ with the mass of the system.

Multiple Choice

1. When the quantity $(m_2 - m_1)$ is increased for an Atwood machine, (a) the acceleration decreases, (b) F is maintained constant, *(c) the total mass may be maintained constant, (d) mass is necessarily added to the system.

2. When the quantity $(m_2 + m_1)$ is maintained constant in the experiment, (a) mass is added and/or removed, (b) the acceleration remains constant for all trials, (c) the system moves with a constant velocity, *(d) the force is varied by transferring mass.

3. If both $(m_2 - m_1)$ and $(m_1 + m_2)$ are varied for each experimental trial, then (a) mass is necessarily added to the system, *(b) it is possible for the acceleration to remain constant, (c) the net force remains constant, (d) the total mass remains constant.

Essay

1. Why should m_f and y be measured for each trial? (Give reasons for possible changes.)

Experiment 8   CONSERVATION OF LINEAR MOMENTUM:
                 THE AIR TRACK

Comments and Hints

    There are a variety of air tracks available, as well
as timing gates and accessories. The instructor may have
to modify specific experimental procedures somewhat to
apply to a particular air track. Also, if electronic timing
gates are used, which provide better accuracy, students
will require instruction on the use of these sensitive
apparatuses.

POST-LAB QUIZ QUESTIONS

Completion

1. The linear momentum of a system is conserved when
    F = 0, the net force acting on the system is zero .

2. In the case of an acceleration, the force acting on an
    object in terms of momentum is equal to $F = \Delta p / \Delta t$,
    time rate of change of momentum .

3. Since p = mv, a particle's momentum is in the same
    direction as its velocity .

4. A massive object moving with a small velocity may have
    the same momentum as an object with a small mass moving
    with a large velocity .

5. The air of an air track acts as a lubricant for the
    gliders to reduce friction.

6. When a glider moves the same distance in equal time
    intervals, it moves with a uniform speed or velocity.

7. When gliders of equal masses approaching each other
    with equal speeds collide, the gliders are stationary
    after collision.

8. When a moving glider of mass m collides with a stationary
    glider of the same mass, after collision the initially
    stationary glider has momentum equal to that of the
    incoming glider .

9. In the case of the preceding Question 7, there is a
    complete transfer of momentum.

10. If a moving glider of small mass collides with a massive,
    stationary glider, after collision the incoming glider
    moves in the opposite direction .

23

Multiple Choice

1. Momentum has units of *(a) kg-m/s, (b) kg-m, (c) g-cm-s, (d) g-cm/s^2.

2. Momentum may also be affected by a change in mass. If an object of mass m and velocity v has a mass of m/4 and a velocity of 2v after a collision, then its momentum is *(a) decreased by one-half, (b) the same, (c) doubled, (d) conserved.

3. Two moving objects may have a total momentum of zero (a) only if they have the same mass, (b) move in the same direction, (c) only if they have the same velocity, *(d) if their momenta are equal and opposite.

4. When two objects of mass m and having equal and opposite velocities collide, (a) they rebound in opposite directions, (b) one transfers all of its momentum to the other and remains stationary, *(c) the total momentum is zero after collision, (d) the total momentum is not conserved.

5. When a moving glider of small mass collides with a stationary glider of large mass, after collision (a) they move in the same direction, (b) the large mass glider remains stationary, (c) the momentum is zero, *(d) they move in opposite directions.

Essay

1. Discuss the relationship between Newton's first law of motion and the conservation of momentum.

Experiment 9   PROJECTILE MOTION: THE BALLISTIC PENDULUM

This experiment is one of the students' favorites. Not only is it enjoyable, but also instructive in that it combines the conservation of linear momentum and the conservation of mechanical energy, as well as application of projectile theory.

Comments and Hints

(a)   Stress safety.   Keep hands clear when the gun is fired and make sure the path is clear in the trajectory procedure so no one gets hit with a projectile.

(b)   Alignment of the pendulum bob and projectile may present and require pendulum adjustment.   Some ballistic pendulum models are more prone to this than others.

(c)   In cocking the gun, the ball and rod both move on some models, while the ball slides over a fixed rod on others.   The latter provides greater alignment, but students may scrape their hands while cocking the gun.   With the moving ball and rod model, the palm of the hand may be used for cocking, while on the stationary rod model, the fingers must be used.   In either case, some students may find this difficult with a strong spring tension.   A strong lab partner usually provides assistance.

(d)   In the Range-Angle of projection portion of the experiment, students quickly learn that some type of obstruction, e.g., a meter stick, will keep the ball from rolling down the aisle after impact.   You may wish to have them mathematically analyze the range for a particular angle of projection.   This is particularly instructive if the apparatus is elevated on a lab stool or table rather than the floor.   A table-top range-angle apparatus is available from Central Scientific Co.   This is essentially an orientable gun (type used on model shown in Fig. 9-1b) with an attached protractor scale.

Answers to Selected Experiment Questions

A.   The Ballistic Pendulum

1.   Inelastic due to frictional energy losses in embedding of the ball.

$$K_i = \tfrac{1}{2}mv_{x_o}^2 \quad \text{and} \quad K_f = \tfrac{1}{2}(m + M)V^2 = (m + M)gh, \text{ and } K_i \neq K_f.$$

2. Fractional energy loss $= 1 - (K_f/K_i) = 1 - \dfrac{(m + M)gh}{\frac{1}{2}mv_{x_o}^2}$

3. Fractional energy loss $= 1 - (K_f/K_i) = \dfrac{p_f^2/2(m + M)}{p_i^2/2m}$

With $p_i = p_f$ (conservation of momentum),

F.E.L. $= 1 - m/(m + M) = (m + M - m)/(m + M) = M/(m + M)$

POST-LAB QUIZ QUESTIONS

Completion

1. During the ball-bob collision ___(linear)___ momentum is conserved.

2. After collision, the linear momentum is not conserved because of the external force of _gravity_.

3. The conservation of mechanical energy is applied to the pendulum system _after_ collision.

(Questions 4-7 as a set) *

If a lighter (less massive) ball were used in the pendulum experiment for a second set of data (with the same gun spring tension):

4. The initial horizontal velocity of the ball would be _greater_.

5. The initial kinetic energy of the ball would be _the same_.

    (Hint: consider the work-energy theorem.)

6. The initial momentum of the lighter ball would be _less_ than that of the heavier ball. (Hint: consider

_____

*Note: Question 7 may be omitted if involved mathematics are too difficult. To show, with $m_2 < m_1$: find v_2/v_1 from K_2/K_1, and then V_2/V_1 with $mv = (m + M)V$. This yields $V_2 > V_1$ and $V = (2gh)^{\frac{1}{2}}$.

26

Exp. 9

$K = p^2/2m.$)

7. For the lighter ball, the pendulum would rise to a _greater_ height.

8. For a horizontal porjection, the greater the initial velocity, the _greater_ the range.

9. For a horizontal projection, the acceleration due to gravity increases the _vertical_ velocity of the projectile.

10. The range of a projectile at an angle of 55° is the same as that of a projectile with the same initial velocity at an angle of _35°_ .

Multiple Choice

1. The ballistic pendulum allows the determination of (a) a projectile's mass, *(b) a projectile's velocity, (c) the acceleration due to gravity, (d) the range of a projectile.

2. The linear momentum is conserved (a) throughout the pendulum action, (b) only before collision, *(c) until the pendulum starts to swing upward, (d) when the pendulum reaches its maximum swing.

3. The conservation of mechanical energy holds (a) throughout the ballistic pendulum procedure, (b) only before collision, (d) during collision, *(d) for the pendulum upswing immediately after collision.

4. The change in the height of the pendulum bob depends on the (a) range, *(b) initial velocity of the projectile, (c) acceleration due to gravity, (d) mass of the bob only.

5. The fractional energy loss during collision (a) depends on the conservation of momentum, (b) is the same for all cases, (c) is independent of the projectile mass, *(d) increases as the projectile mass increases.

6. For a horizontal projection, which of the following is constant? *(a) v_{x_o}, (b) v_y, (c) the vertical momentum, (d) the kinetic energy.

7. For a horizontal projection, the range of the projectile depends on (a) the initial velocity only, (b) the final vertical velocity, *(c) the distance of fall, (d) the mass of the projectile.

8. The range of a projectile at an arbitrary angle θ, where θ is less than 45°, is the same (a) for all angles, (b) as for 45°, (c) as for $(45^\circ + \theta)$, *(d) as for $(90^\circ - \theta)$.

Essay

1. Discuss and show explicitly the effects of changing the mass of the projectile of the ballistic pendulum on (a) initial velocity, (b) momentum, (c) kinetic energy, (d) fractional energy loss, and (e) height of pendulum rise.

2. Suppose a projectile were fired at an angle θ above the horizontal from a table top and landed on the floor. Would the angle for maximum range be 45°? Justify your answer.

Experiment 10 CENTRIPETAL FORCE

Comments and Hints

A. Motorized Apparatus

Safety is the main consideration here. Make certain
the rotor is fastened securely to the rotating arm by means
of the finger screw. It is advisable to have students
wear safety glasses for protection from any object flying
off the rotating apparatus due to a lack of centripetal
force. Excessive speeds should be avoided. Also, students
should be cautioned to keep hands and long hair away from
the rotor.

As pointed out in the experiment, a belt guard should
always be used for the nonself-contained model.

B. Manual Apparatus

A major consideration here is practice in rotating
the rotor so as to achieve a fairly constant rotational
speed.

Answers to Selected Experiment Questions

2. With $F_c = 4\pi^2 m r f^2$ (Eq. 10-3),

   (a) if F_c is increased, say doubled ($F_2 = 2F_1$), with
   r constant, then $(f_2/f_1)^2 = F_2/F_1 = 2$, and

   $f_2 = (2)^{\frac{1}{2}} f_1 = (1.41) f_1$.

   (b) if f and r are free to vary, then the product of rf^2
        must increase so as to equal the increased centri-
        petal force, and r and f can vary accordingly.

3. Adding the counter differences for five 1-min consecutive
    counter intervals as would be done in an averaging process:

    $\sum \Delta n_i = \Delta n_1 + \Delta n_2 + \Delta n_3 + \Delta n_4 + \Delta n_5$

    $= (n_1 - n_o) + (n_2 - n_1) + (n_3 - n_2) + (n_4 - n_3) +$

    $(n_5 - n_4) = n_5 - n_o$

But, $n_5 - n_0$ is just the difference between the counter readings at t_5 = 5 min and t_0 = 0, which is simply the count of one 5-min time interval.

POST-LAB QUIZ QUESTIONS

Completion

1. For an object in uniform circular motion, a __centripetal force (acceleration)__ is required.

2. The centripetal acceleration of an object in circular motion is directly proportional to the __square__ of its orbital speed.

3. The greater the orbit for an object in uniform circular motion at a particular speed, the __less__ centripetal force is required.

4. In the experimental apparatus, the centripetal force is supplied by __a spring (force)__.

5. Given two masses, one 4 times more massive as the other (m_2 = $4m_1$), in circular orbit at the same radius and with the same centripetal force. Then, the rotational frequency f_1 of m_1 is __twice__ that of m_2.

6. The velocity of an object in uniform circular motion is not constant because of a __change in direction__.

Multiple Choice

1. An object in uniform circular motion has an acceleration (a) of zero, (b) directed tangentially, (c) directed outwardly, *(d) directed inwardly.

2. If the orbital speed of an object in circular motion (constant r) is increased 3-fold, the required centripetal force is how many times as great? (a) the same, (b) 3, (c) 6, *(d) 9.

3. If the centripetal force of an object in uniform circular motion goes suddenly to zero, the object moves in a path *(a) tangential to the circular orbit, (b) radially outward, (c) radially inward, (d) the same as before.

4. When the angular frequency of the rotor in the experiment is increased, (a) the radius of the orbit decreases, *(b) the spring force increases, (d) the centripetal force increases by the same proportion, (d) there is no change in the orbital speed.

5. If an object in circular motion at radius r and speed v has its radius increased 4-fold, for the same centripetal force, its speed would (a) decrease by one-half, (b) remain the same, *(c) double, (d) increase by a factor of 4.

Essay

1. Discuss the orbital motion of an object that has both centripetal acceleration and tangential acceleration.

Experiment 11 FRICTION

Comments and Hints

The experiment is straight forward and shows how variable the general empirical "rules" of friction can be. A major source of error is in getting the block to move with a uniform velocity because of variations in the plane's surface. Suggested experimental technique calls for using one portion of the plane, viz., the middle, for experimental observations to minimize variations. The block may speed up or slow down elsewhere on the plane.

Answers to Selected Experiment Questions

4. Summing the forces on the block (F = ma),

$$mg \sin\theta - \mu_k N = mg \sin\theta - \mu_k mg \cos\theta = ma = 0 \text{ (constant v)}$$

and $\quad \mu_k = \sin\theta / \cos\theta = \tan\theta$

5. Summing the forces on the block (F = ma), where M is the suspended mass and m the mass of the block,

$$mg - mg \sin\theta - \mu_k mg \cos\theta = ma = 0 \quad \text{(constant v)}$$

and

$$mg(\sin\theta + \mu_k \cos\theta) = Mg$$

or $\quad \sin\theta + \mu_k \cos\theta = M/m$

POST-LAB QUIZ QUESTIONS

Completion

1. An empirical rule states that the frictional force is <u>independent</u> of the surface area of contact.

2. The ratio of the friction force f and the normal force on an object is called the <u>coefficient of friction</u>.

3. For the relationship, $f_s = \mu_s N$, the static force of friction has its <u>maximum</u> value.

4. The value of a coefficient of friction depends on the _nature_ and _roughness_ of the surfaces.

5. For a mass on an inclined plane, the magnitude of the normal force on the mass is equal to _mg cosθ_.

6. The coefficient of friction has _no_ units.

7. When an object slides on a surface with a constant velocity, the force of kinetic friction is _balanced by an equal and opposite force_ .

8. A horizontal force is applied to a stationary block. The block will move when this force F is slightly greater than $f_s = \mu_s N$.

Multiple Choice

1. The coefficient of friction (a) has units of force, (b) is always less than one, (c) is equal to N, *(d) is defined by f/N.

2. The force of friction is (a) dependent on the surface area of contact, *(b) proportional to the normal component of the force acting on an object, (c) is unitless, (d) depends on the sliding speed.

3. The coefficient of static friction (a) is the same as μ_k, (b) is equal to N/f_s, *(c) is generally greater than μ_k for a given pair of surfaces, (d) has a maximum value when $f_s = \mu_s N$.

4. When a block slides down an inclined plane with a constant velocity, (a) there is a net force on the block, *(b) the magnitude of the frictional force is proportional to mg cosθ , (c) the friction is zero, (d) the normal force is zero.

5. When a block slides down an inclined plane with a constant velocity, *(a) $f_k = N \tan \theta$, (b) $f_s < \mu_s N$, (c) the plane must be polished, (d) a lubricant is required.

Essay

1.   Discuss the validity of the empirical rules of friction
     based on your experimental results.

2.   As shown in the experiment, $\mu_k = \tan\theta$. Describe the
     physical significance of the conditions of (a)$\theta = 0$, and
     (b) θ approaching 90°.

Experiment 12 WORK AND ENERGY

Comments and Hints

As is often the case, students seem to not understand what they are measuring in the experiment. It is suggested that the theory section be covered thoroughly to insure an understanding of the two experimental methods of measuring the work of friction.

One common experimental error is the measurement of the angle of the incline. Some students have a problem reading a protractor, and if an inclined plane with an attached scale is used (as in Fig. 12-2b), the top of the marker is often used as the reference line rather than the bottom of the marker. In the latter case, have the students drop the plane to the horizontal position and have them note where the zero reading is indicated.

Answers to Selected Experiment Questions

2.   (a) and (b). $\sum F = ma = 0$ (constant velocity)

3.   Net work = 0, since net force is zero.

5.   Summing forces,

$$m_c g \sin\theta - \mu m_c g \cos\theta - m_2 g = ma = 0 \text{ (constant velocity)}$$

and $\mu = \sin\theta/\cos\theta - m_2/m_c \cos\theta = \tan\theta - m_2/m_c \cos\theta$

POST-LAB QUIZ QUESTIONS

Completion

1.   A system with friction is __nonconservative__ .

2.   The work of friction is given by the frictional force times the __distance (traveled)__ .

3.   When a car moves up an inclined plane, the change in height gives rise to an increase in __potential energy__ .

4.   In the energy method in the experiment, the kinetic energy does not come into account because __there is no change in the KE (constant v)__ .

5. Since the car moves at a constant speed, the net force is zero, and hence, so is the net work .

Multiple Choice

1. In a nonconservative system, which of the following is conserved? (a) kinetic energy, (b) potential energy, (c) mechanical energy, *(d) total energy.

2. For a car moving on an inclined plane with a constant speed, (a) the system is conservative, *(b) the net work is zero, (c) a net force acts on the car, (d) the work of friction exceeds the change in potential energy.

3. For a car accelerating on an inclined plane, (a) the net work is zero, (b) there is no friction work, *(c) there is a change in kinetic energy, (d) the mechanical energy is conserved.

Experiment 13   TORQUES, EQUILIBRIUM, AND CENTER OF GRAVITY

Comments and Hints

This experiment allows students to obtain a hands-on, basic understanding of torque and the conditions of equilibrium. In particular, the apparatus in part B with two points of support permits a more detailed investigation of the force equilibrium condition, $\int F = 0$.

In suspending the masses from the meter stick in any case, the author prefers the string loop method because of its simplicity, ease of reading mass location, and being able to suspend a mass from the zero end of the meter stick (with the help of a bit of masking tape).

Common student difficulties arise from taking the meter stick position or reading of a suspended mass as the moment arm, rather than the distance of the mass from the axis of rotation. Some students have difficulty in Part A in understanding the concept of linear mass density and the mass contributions of portions of the meter stick.

Answers to Selected Experiment Questions

1.   The downward weight force is balanced by the upward reaction force of the support on the stick.

4.   Yes. The mass m_3 would require a moment arm of 90 cm or 40 cm beyond the end of the meter stick (with the center of mass at the 50 cm position). The problem could be resolved by using a 2-meter stick.

5.   No. If the support points are not equidistant, there may be some angle considerations, but the conditions of equilibrium would still hold under the appropriate conditions.

POST-LAB QUIZ QUESTIONS

1.   The condition for translational equilibrium is $\underline{\int F = 0}$.

2.   The condition for rotational equilibrium is $\underline{\int \tau = 0}$.

3.   The conditions for mechanical equilibrium are $\underline{\int F = 0}$ and $\underline{\int \tau = 0}$.

4. For a constant force with a line of action perpendicular to a body's axis of rotation, the torque varies with the moment (lever) arm .

5. In rotational equilibrium, the sum of the counterclockwise torques equals the sum of the clockwise torques.

6. A body's center of gravity is defined by gravitational torques.

7. The sum of the gravitational torques about an axis through a body's center of gravity is equal to zero.

8. In a uniform gravitational field (g is constant), the center of mass coincides with the location of the center of gravity .

9. For a symmetric, uniform object, the center of gravity is located at its center of symmetry .

10. Two equal and opposite forces act on a meter stick at equidistant positions on opposite sides of its center of mass. In this case, $\sum F$ = 0 and $\sum \tau$ ≠ 0 .

Multiple Choice

1. Another name for torque is (a) moment arm, *(b) moment of force, (c) momentum of equilibrium, (d) center of gravity.

2. Another name for the moment arm of a torque is *(a) lever arm, (b) balancing arm, (c) moment of force, (d) equilibrium arm.

3. If all the forces acting on a body act through its axis of rotation, then (a) there is a net moment of force, (b) the center of gravity lies outside the body, (c) $\sum F = 0$, *(d) $\sum \tau = 0$.

4. A necessary condition for mechanical equilibrium is (a) that the torque lever arms equal zero, (b) that the forces are concurrent (act through the same point), *(c) translational equilibrium, (d) that the sum of the clockwise lever arms equal the sum of the counterclockwise lever arms.

5. For a uniform meter stick supported at its center of gravity with a mass of 100 grams suspended at the 20 cm position, the maximum mass that can be suspended on the opposite side of the center of gravity no closer than 1 cm from the support point is (a) 100 gm, (b) 300 gm, (c) 900 gm, *(d) 3 kg.

6. For the situation in the previous question, the smallest mass that could be suspended on the opposite side of the center of mass would be *(a) 60 gm, (b) 70 gm, (c) 80 gm, (d) 120 gm.

Essay

1. Do the conditions for mechanical equilibrium require that a body be in static equilibrium? Explain in detail.

Experiment 14 SIMPLE MACHINES:
              MECHANICAL ADVANTAGE AND EFFICIENCY

Comments and Hints

    This experiment in effect reviews the concepts of
work and energy, and real and ideal systems. It may be
used as a good "fill-in" or review experiment without specific
class coverage of machines. Also, a good understanding
of mechanical efficiency helps a great deal when later
studying thermal efficiency.

    A couple of common student difficulties in the experiment
are: a problem in recognizing the equivalence of block
pulleys (common axis) and tandem pulleys (individual sheave
axes) when both are available, and a problem in getting
strings wrapped around the wheel and axle. A bit of explanation helps in the former and a bit of masking tape
helps in the latter.

Answers to Selected Experiment Questions

5(b). The number of supporting strands contribute equally
       to d_o. For example, suppose there are 5 support strands.
       For a d_i = 5 cm, then each support strand is shortened by
       1 cm, which is also d_o, and TMA = d_i/d_o = 5/1 = 5.

7.   Let R = 5.0 cm and r = 0.50 cm, and with F_i = 2.0 N,
           F_o/F_i = R/r = 5.0/0.50 = 10
       and F_o = $10F_i$ = (10)(2.0) = 20 N

POST-LAB QUIZ QUESTIONS

Completion

1. A machine is a device that changes the magnitude (and/or)
    direction of a force.

2. The ratio of a machine's output force and input force
    is called its AMA .

3. In no case is work multiplied by a machine.

4. For a machine, the total work input is equal to the
    useful work done plus the work done against friction.

5. The TMA of a machine is always greater than its AMA.

40

6. The ratio of the useful work output and the total work input is called the efficiency .

7. In terms of the AMA and TMA, efficiency is equal to AMA/TMA .

8. In terms of the angle of incline, the TMA of an inclined plane is equal to $1/\sin\theta$.

9. A pulley system with 4 supporting strands would have a TMA of 4 .

10. If the axle of a wheel and axle has a larger radius than the wheel, then there is a force reduction .

Multiple Choice

1. Which one of the following does not take friction into account? (a) AMA, *(b) TMA, (c) efficiency, (d) useful work.

2. A machine is basically (a) a work multiplier, (b) an efficiency multiplier, (c) a TMA multiplier, *(d) a force multiplier.

3. The ratio of F_o/F_i is the *(a) AMA, (b) TMA, (c) efficiency, (d) useful work.

4. The ratio of the input force distance and the output force distance is the (a) AMA, *(b) TMA, (c) efficiency, (d) total work.

5. Which one of the following can be determined from the geometry of a machine? (a) AMA, *(b) TMA, (c) efficiency, (d) F_o/F_i.

6. The ratio of the work output and the work input of a machine is its (a) AMA, (b) TMA, *(c) efficiency, (d) force multiplication.

7. The TMA of an inclined plane is given by (a) h_i/h_o, (b) $\sin\theta$, *(c) L/H, (d) R/r.

8. A machine that is equivalent to a lever with equal lever arms is a *(a) pulley, (b) inclined plane, (c) wheel and axle, (d) wedge.

9. Which one of the following is sometimes classified as an inclined plane? (a) pulley, (b) lever, *(c) screw, (d) wheel and axle.

10. The TMA of a wheel and axle with a wheel radius of 50 cm and an axle radius of 2 cm is (a) 5, (b) 10, *(c) 25, (d) 50.

Essay

1. Discuss the operation of a machine in terms of the conservation of energy.

2. What are the implications of an efficiency (a) equal to one, and (b) greater than one? Can these conditions occur?

Experiment 15   ROTATIONAL MOTION AND MOMENT OF INERTIA

Comments and Hints

There are various types of inertia apparatus, so some variations may have to be made in the experimental procedures. Excessive rotational speeds should be avoided. Care should be given to alignment and balance of the rotating members. Students should be cautioned about keeping clear of the rotating objects and to be careful not to drop a heavy object on a foot.

Answers to Selected Experiment Questions

A1 (and B1). $\tau_f = m_o g r$, and

$$E_{lost} = m_o g y = \tau_f y/r = \tau_f \theta, \text{ since } y/r = \theta.$$

A2.   With $\tau_a = I \alpha + \tau_f$ $(y = ax + b)$,

(a) $b = 0$ or $\tau_f = 0$. No friction.

(b) $-b$ or $-\tau_f$. Implies that friction contributes to the applied torque.

B2. $I = \frac{1}{2}MR^2$

(a)   O': $I = I_d + I_{c'}$, where $I_{c'} = I_{cm} + Md^2 = \frac{1}{2}M_c r^2 + M_c d^2$

and $I = \frac{1}{2}M_d R^2 + \frac{1}{2}M_c r^2 + M_c d^2$

(b)   O: $I = I_c + I_{d'} = \frac{1}{2}M_c r^2 + \frac{1}{2}M_d R^2 + M_d d^2$

POST-LAB QUIZ QUESTIONS

Completion

1.   The moment of inertia of a body depends on its mass <u>distribution</u> and <u>shape</u>.

2.   In terms of the mass particles of a body, the moment of inertia I is equal to <u>$\sum_i m_i r_i^2$</u>.

3. The applied torque on a rotating disk is equal to the opposing frictional torque when $\underline{\alpha = 0 \text{ (constant } \omega \text{)}}$.

4. The rotational analog of Newton's second law (F = ma) is $\underline{\tau = I\alpha}$.

5. Rotational kinetic energy is given by the relationship $\underline{\frac{1}{2}I\omega^2}$.

6. The moment of inertia of a body about an axis parallel to an axis through its center of mass differs from the moment of inertia about the center of mass axis by a factor of $\underline{Md^2}$.

7. If objects are stacked on each other so that their centers of mass coincide, the moment of inertia of the combination about an axis through the centers of mass is equal to $\underline{I = I_1 + I_2 + I_3 + \dots}$.

Multiple Choice

1. The unit of angular acceleration is usually given as rad/s^2, but technically is (a) rad, (b) s, (c) 1/s, *(d) s^{-2}.

2. The unit of torque in the SI system is *(a) N-m, (b) N/s^2, (c) kg-m/s, (d) J-s.

3. If the net torque on a body is zero, then (a) it is accelerated, (b) the net force must be zero, *(c) the angular velocity is constant, (d) the moment of inertia is zero.

4. The moment of inertia (a) does not depend on the shape of an object, *(b) may have different values about different axes, (c) has units of kg-m, (d) is the rotational analog of momentum.

5. A 1-kg cylinder has a moment of inertia of 0.50 kg-m^2 about an axis through its center of mass. The moment of inertia about a parallel axis 30 cm away is

    *(a) 0.59 kg-m^2, (b) 0.67 kg-m^2, (c) 0.75 kg-m^2,

    (d) 1.4 kg-m^2.

Experiment 16 ELASTICITY: YOUNG'S MODULUS

Comments and Hints

Students are surprised to find that a steel wire has appreciable elasticity. Measurement of the change in length by the optical lever method is more sensitive and gives students an introduction to this method, while the micrometer method is simpler but less sensitive.

Answers to Selected Experiment Questions

1. (a) and (b). The Young's modulus relationship is valid for any wire segment and for various initial conditions.

5. (a) $L_o' = 2L_o$ and $\Delta L' = \Delta L$, then

$$F' = (L_o/L_o')F_o = F_o/2$$

(b) $d' = 2d_o$, $A_o = \pi d_o^2/4$, and $A' = 4A_o$. Then, with

$$L_o' = L_o \text{ and } \Delta L' = \Delta L,$$
$$F' = (A'/A_o)F_o = 4F_o$$

6. Referring to the figure,

$$\Theta_r + \beta + \Theta = \Theta_r' + \alpha + \beta$$

and $\alpha = \Theta + \Theta_r - \Theta_r'$

But, $\Theta_i - \Theta_i' = \Theta = \Theta_r - \Theta_r'$

so $\alpha = 2\Theta$

POST-LAB QUIZ QUESTIONS

Completion

1. If a deformed body tends to return to its original dimensions, it is said to be elastic .

2. The deformation or relative change in the dimensions or shape of a body subject to stress is expressed in terms of strain ($\Delta L/L_o$) .

3. An elastic modulus is the ratio of stress/strain .

4. The product of Young's modulus and the strain is equal to the (tensile) stress .

5. The greater the cross sectional area of a wire, the greater the load required for a given length change.

6. The longer the initial length of a stressed wire, the smaller the load for a given length change.

7. The SI unit of tensile strain is none (unitless) .

8. The SI unit of tensile stress is N/m^2 (Pa) .

9. A material for which the stress is directly proportional to the strain is said to obey Hooke's law .

10. If the stress exceeds the elastic limit of a material, when the stress is removed the object is permanently strained or deformed .

Multiple Choice

1. The elasticity of a material is characterized by (a) strain, (b) stress, (c) elastic limit, *(d) elastic modulus.

2. Tensile stress is equal to (a) $\Delta L/L_o$, *(b) F/A, (c) Y, (d) YA/L_o.

3. The SI unit of tensile stress is *(a) N/m^2, (b) N-m, (c) $kg-m/s^2$, (d) none (unitless).

4. The SI unit of tensile strain is (a) N/m^2, (b) m^2, (c) m, *(d) none (unitless).

5. Young's modulus has the SI unit *(a) N/m^2, (b) $kg-m^2$, (c) $1/m^2$, (d) none (unitless).

6. An object is permanently deformed when the applied stress exceeds the material's (a) Young's modulus, (b)elastic lag, *(c) elastic limit, (d) optical lever.

7. On a stress vs. strain plot, the slope of the initial linear portion of the graph is equal to (a) the value of the stress at the elastic limit, *(b) Young's modulus, (c) the value of the stress at the breaking point, (d) zero.

8. The greater the Young's modulus of a wire, *(a) the smaller the fractional length change for a given stress, (b) the smaller the slope on a stress vs. strain graph, (c) the less the stress required for a given strain, (d) the greater the stress of its breaking point.

Essay

1. Referring to Appendix Table A2, discuss the elasticity and uses of wires made from the various metals.

Experiment 17   HOOKE'S LAW AND SIMPLE HARMONIC MOTION

Comments and Hints

   The experiment is straight forward and provides a good exercise in the study of Hooke's law and simple harmonic motion. The elongation of a rubber band demonstrates that all elastic materials do not follow Hooke's law.

Answers to Selected Experiment Questions

1.   (a)   The initial displacement force, $F_o = ky_o$.

4.   (a) $y = 10 \cos 2\pi t/T$ cm   (b) $y = 8 \sin 2\pi t/T$ cm

   (c) $y = -12 \sin 2\pi t/T$ cm

5.   (a) $y = 10 \cos 2\pi(T/2)/T = -10$ cm

   (b) $y = 10 \cos 2\pi(3T/2)/T = -10$ cm

   (c) $y = 10 \cos 2\pi(3T)/T = 10$ cm

POST-LAB QUIZ QUESTIONS

Completion

1.   Hooke's law states that the restoring force is pro-portional to the displacement .

2.   In the equation, $F = -kx$, for a spring, the k is the spring constant .

3.   The greater the spring constant, the stronger or stiffer the spring.

4.   A particle in motion under the influence of a force described by Hooke's law undergoes SHM .

5.   The spring constant k has the SI unit of N/m .

6.   When the motion of an object is repeated at regular intervals, its motion is periodic (or harmonic) .

7.   Sine and cosine functions are called harmonic functions.

8.   In the equation, $y = A \cos 2\pi t/T$, the A is the amplitude .

9. The amplitude of an object in SHM is determined by the initial or maximum displacement .

10. When the amplitude of SHM decreases with time, the motion is said to be damped .

Multiple Choice

1. All materials (a) obey Hooke's law, (b) describe SHM when vibrating, *(c) are elastic to some degree, (d) have a restoring force proportional to the deformation.

2. The maximum displacement of an object in SHM is called the *(a) amplitude, (b) period, (c) frequency, (d) spring constant.

3. A mass on a spring is pulled down a distance of 5 cm and released. Its motion is described by
    (a) $y = 5 \cos 2\pi t/T$,   *(b) $y = -5 \cos 2\pi t/T$,
    (c) $y = 5 \sin 2\pi t/T$,   (d) $y = -5 \sin 2\pi t/T$.

4. A mass hanging on a spring is given a sharp downward impulse force. The general resulting motion is described by (a) $y = A \cos 2\pi t/T$, (b) $y = -A \cos 2\pi t/T$,
    (c) $y = A \sin 2\pi t/T$,   *(d) $y = -A \sin 2\pi t/T$.

5. The greater the spring constant of an oscillating spring, (a) the greater the amplitude, (b) the greater the period, *(c) the more oscillations per second, (d) the more it follows SHM.

Experiment 18   STANDING WAVES IN A STRING

Comments and Hints

The vibrating string provides a hands-on experience of standing waves for students. The number of harmonics that can be obtained depends on several factors, viz., the vibrator itself and the type of string used. The former is inherent, but you may wish to experiment with the latter.

It is found that although the vibrator frequency is theoretically 120 Hz, there may be an occasional 60 Hz vibrator-string resonance. This leads to scattered data points (see Experiment Question 2).

Answers to Selected Experiment Questions

1. (a) $\ell_1 = \lambda/2 = L/2$, so $L = \lambda$ and from $L = n\,\lambda/2$, by inspection $n = 2$ or the second harmonic.

3. (a) one, (b) one

POST-LAB QUIZ QUESTIONS

Completion

1. The wavelength is __inversely__ proportional to the frequency.

2. The superposition of two waves of equal amplitude and frequency traveling in opposite directions produces a _standing (stationary) wave_.

3. A stationary point of a standing wave is called a _node_.

4. Points of maximum displacement of a standing wave are called _antinodes_.

5. For a standing wave in a string of length L, the wavelength of the fundamental frequency is equal to _2L_.

6. Only an integral number of _half wavelengths_ may "fit" into the length L of a string for standing waves.

7. The wave speed of a wave in a particular stretched string increases with _increased tension_.

Exp. 18

8.   Only certain frequencies produce standing waves for
      a given string <u>tension</u>, <u>density</u>, and <u>length</u>.

9.   The lowest natural frequency is called the <u>fundamental
      frequency</u>.

10.   The third harmonic has <u>three</u> loops or half-wavelengths
      in a vibrating string.

Multiple Choice

1.   The period of a wave cycle is equal to (a) f, *(b) λ/v,
      (c) the fundamental frequency, (d) the mass density.

2.   A standing wave results from *(a) periodic interference,
      (b) amplitude, (c) increased wavelengths, (d) nodes.

3.   A string with a standing wave may be grasped at what
      position without completely destroying the standing
      wave pattern? (a) maximum amplitude, (b) antinode,
      *(c) node, (d) any position.

4.   A string of length L vibrates at its third harmonic
      frequency. The string could be grasped at what position
      without completely destroying the standing wave pattern?
      (a) L/4, (b) L/2, (c) L/8, *(d) L/3.

5.   Which one of the following normal nodes has the greatest
      wave speed? (a) f_1, (b) f_2, (c) f_3, *(d) f_4

Essay

1.   Discuss the standing waves in the strings of stringed
      musical instruments and how different musical notes are
      produced.

Experiment 19   AIR COLUMN RESONANCE: THE SPEED OF SOUND IN AIR

Comments and Hints

This is another well-received and instructive experiment. Students are generally surprised and fascinated on being able to audibly detect resonance conditions.

There are two types of resonance tube apparatus available. One has a glass tube and the other has a plastic tube. Both work equally well.   The glass tubes are steadier, but more expensive and prone to breakage. Each apparatus has the common problem of springing a leak around the bottom seal -- glass-to-metal in one case and plastic-to-rubber in the other.   This can usually be repaired with a waterproof sealant.   It is recommended that the water be removed from the apparatus by yourself or a trained lab assistant after the experiment to minimize mishandling that may cause seal leaks and the breakage of glass tubes (if this type is used).

Answers to Selected Experiment Questions

1.   Yes.   With a fixed fork frequency, an increase in temperature increases the speed of sound and affects (increases) the wavelength ($\lambda f = v$).   This would affect the measured tube lengths.

2.   With $f_n = nv/4L$, $n = 1,3,5,....$, and L and v constant,

   $f'_n = (n'/n)f_n$ and for n = 1, then $f'_n = n'f_1$.

   (a)   No. A fork with a lower frequency would not resonate since its greater wavelength would not "fit in" L_1.

   (b)   Yes. A fork with a higher frequency would produce resonances of higher harmonics, n' = 3.5,... and

      $f'_3 = 3f_1$, $f'_5 = 5f_1$, etc.

4.   (a)   For example, for n = 1, then $L_1 = \lambda/4$ and $\lambda = v/f$ from which the theoretical or actual L_1 may be calculated.   Then, $E = L_1 - L_{meas}$.

Exp. 19

POST-LAB QUIZ QUESTIONS

1. The resonance condition may be detected audibly when there is an antinode near the open end of the tube.

2. The second harmonic is equivalent to the first overtone.

3. The wavelength segment that "fits in" the tube for the second harmonic is $3\lambda/4$.

4. At a resonance condition, there must be a node at the closed (water) end of the tube.

5. The three experimental parameters involved in the resonance condition of an air column are f, L, and v_s (speed of sound) .

6. The wavelength difference between two successive audible resonance conditions is $\lambda/2$.

7. The speed of sound increases with increasing air temperature.

8. For resonance in an open organ pipe, there are antinodes at each end of the tube.

9. The fundamental frequency corresponds to n = 1 .

10. At resonance condition, there is maximum energy transfer.

Multiple Choice

1. Which of the following is not a resonance condition for a closed pipe? (a) $\lambda/4$, (b) $3\lambda/4$, *(c) λ , (d) $5\lambda/4$.

2. The third natural frequency of an oscillator is called the (a) fundamental frequency, (b) second harmonic, (c) third overtone, *(d) third harmonic.

3. In the experiment, the effective tube length is varied so as to find the appropriate (a) f, *(b) λ , (c) v_s, (d) end correction.

4. More resonance positions can be observed for a tube of a given length if *(a) a fork of higher frequency is used, (b) the air temperature is increased, (c) the diameter of the tube is increased, (d) the water level is lowered more quickly.

5. A required condition for resonance in the experimental air column was (a) that the temperature be 20°C, (b) the diameter of the tube be less than 5 cm, (c) the fundamental frequency have a tube length of $\lambda /2$, *(d) that there be a node at the closed end.

Essay

1. Discuss the differences in the resonance conditions for an open organ pipe and a closed organ pipe.

2. Do all vibrating systems have one or more overtones? Explain.

Experiment 20   THE GAS LAWS

Comments and Hints

The proper handling of mercury is the major consideration in this experiment. Mercury is cumulative toxic if the vapor is inhaled and mercury has an appreciable vapor pressure at normal temperatures. Mercury is known to produce nervous system disorders when inhaled over long periods. (You may wish to relate the story of the Mad Hatter in Lewis Carroll's <u>Alice in Wonderland</u> being "mad" presumably due to mercury poisoning. In the hatting industry when beaver skin hats were in fashion, the beaver pelts were treated with mercury compounds. It was common for workers after long exposure to be "mad as a hatter" with nervous disorders.)

However, mercury can be used safely if handled properly. Be particularly careful with any mercury spills. These should be cleaned up immediately and there should be no student playing with drops of "quick silver". The handling of mercury with the bare fingers may cause skin irritations and there is a possibility of absorption through the skin. Mercury droplets getting into cracks and crevices give rise to inhalation dangers.

New apparatus with self-contained mercury reservoirs are recommended. However, in any case, care should be taken when transferring and using mercury in the experiment. Should a spill occur, mercury is difficult to collect. One suggestion is to spray the surface with water then wipe with a damp plastic sponge in order to pick up small droplets of mercury. Another is to cover the spill area with flowers of (powdered) sulfur. The sulfur reacts with the mercury to form a protective coating and the droplets may be swept up with the sulfur, particularly from cracks.

For further information, consult the Laboratory Safety References given in the back of this Resource Manual.

Answers to Selected Experiment Questions

1.   (a) $k = pV = (N/m^2)(m^3) = N\text{-}m$

(b) $k' = \dfrac{(h_2 - h_1) + p_a}{x} = (h_3 - h_1)\ [(h_2 - h_1) + p_a]$
$= (mm)\ [\ mm\ ]\ = mm^2$

since p_a is in mm (Hg).

Post-LAB QUIZ QUESTIONS

Completion

1. Boyle's law states that the pressure of a gas at a given temperature is __inversely__ proportional to its volume.

2. The graph of p versus 1/V for a gas at a constant temperature is a __straight line__.

3. For an open tube manometer, the pressure reading is the sum of the __p_g (gauge pressure)__ and __P_a (atmospheric pressure)__

4. Pressure is often expressed in units of mercury length __or mm Hg (torr)__.

5. According to Charles' law, the pressure of a fixed volume of gas increases with __an increase__ in temperature.

6. The temperature in the perfect gas law is __absolute__ temperature.

7. For a constant volume of gas, every degree Celsius change in temperature results in a fractional pressure change of __1/273__ of its pressure at 0^oC.

8. The temperature corresponding to a volume of gas with zero pressure is __absolute zero__.

9. An ideal or perfect gas remains a gas at __any (all)__ temperature(s).

10. According to the perfect gas law, the pressure of a gas depends on its volume, temperature, and __mass (number of molecules)__.

Multiple Choice

1. Boyle's law expresses the relationship between a gas' (a) pressure and temperature, (b) volume and temperature, *(c) volume and pressure, (d) temperature and mass.

2. The difference in the heights of the columns in an open tube manometer gives the (a) total pressure, *(b) gauge pressure, (c) atmospheric pressure, (d) pressure of a confined gas.

3. According to Charles' law, the pressure of a volume of gas would go to zero at a temperature of (a) $0^{\circ}C$, (b) $0^{\circ}F$, (c) 273 K, *(d) $-273^{\circ}C$.

4. The pressure of a gas could be increased by (a) increasing the volume alone, (b) decreasing its temperature alone, (c) increasing the volume and decreasing the temperature, *(d) increasing the mass or amount of gas.

5. If the temperature of a quantity of gas is decreased, then (a) the pressure must decrease, (b) the volume must decrease, (c) the pressure must remain constant, *(d) the product of the pressure and volume must decrease.

Essay

1. Discuss how absolute zero is defined and its significance.

Experiment 21   THE COEFFICIENT OF LINEAR EXPANSION

Comments and Hints

As suggested in the experiment, for convenience and to minimize the number of metal rods needed, lab groups may exchange jacketed rods after making measurements. Of course, the initial lengths (L_o) must also be exchanged.

Because of the relatively small magnitude of ΔL, the largest ΔT is desirable. Taking T_o at room temperature is most convenient, however, you may wish to expand the temperature interval by first putting the rods in ice water. In this case, the L_o must be measured <u>quickly</u> or some special means devised to measure this lower L_o.

Answers to Selected Experiment Questions

2. The values would be different since ΔT would have a different magnitude ($1^{\circ}F$) = $1.8^{\circ}C$). That is,

$\Delta T (1/^{\circ}C)(1.8^{\circ}C/1^{\circ}F) = 1.8\Delta T (1/^{\circ}F)$, which would make α smaller in magnitude, $\alpha \sim 1/\Delta T$.

3. In heating the thermometer tube, the thermal expansion first increases the diameter of the capillary bore and the mercury column drops slightly.

6. From Appendix Table A3, $\alpha = 3.3 \times 10^{-6} \ ^{\circ}C^{-1}$ for Pyrex,

and V_o = 200 ml, $\Delta T = 100^{\circ}C$. With $V = V_o(1 + 3\alpha\Delta T)$, or

$\Delta V = 3\alpha V_o\Delta T = 3(3.3 \times 10^{-6})(10^2) = 9.9 \times 10^{-6}$ ml

POST-LAB QUIZ QUESTIONS

Completion

1. A contraction resulting from a temperature decrease is called a <u>negative</u> expansion.

2. If the thermal expansion is the same in all directions, the expansion is said to be <u>isotropic</u> .

3. $\Delta L/L_o$ is the <u>fractional</u> change in length.

4. The unit of the coefficient of linear expansion is <u>$1/T$ $(1/^{\circ}C)$</u> .

5. The coefficient of linear expansion is __inversely__ proportional to the temperature change.

6. To first order approximation, the coefficient of area expansion has the units $1/T$ ($1/^{\circ}C$) .

7. To first order approximation, the coefficient of volume expansion is equal to 3α .

8. The volume coefficient of expansion to first order approximation has units $1/T$ ($1/^{\circ}C$) .

9. The coefficient of linear expansion is __directly__ proportional to the fractional length change.

10. If in the experiment T_o were the temperature of the rod in the steam jacket and L_o its length at this temperature, a decrease in temperature to room temperature would result in an α of the __same__ value as the same temperature increase process.

Multiple Choice

1. The units of $\Delta L/L_o$ are (a) $1/cm$, (b) cm, (c) cm^3, *(d) none (unitless).

2. L_o is the length of a rod at a temperature (a) T, (b) ΔT, *(c) T_o, (d) near $100^{\circ}C$.

3. The quantity $(L/L_o) - 1$ is equivalent to *(a) $\Delta L/L_o$, (b) ΔL, (c) L_o, (d) 3α .

4. If for a given rod the temperature change ΔT were only one-half that used in the experiment, then α would be (a) one-half as great, (b) twice as great, (c) much smaller, *(d) the same.

5. The greater the α of a material, (a) the smaller ΔL for an increased temperature change, (b) the smaller ΔL for a decreased temperature change, *(c) the greater its area coefficient of expansion, (d) the greater an L_o for a given $\Delta L/\Delta T$.

6. The unit of the volume coefficient expansion to first order approximation is
*(a) $1/^{\circ}C$, (b) $1/^{\circ}C^2$, (c) $1/^{\circ}C^3$, (d) none (unitless).

Essay

1. Discuss the importance of the coefficients of expansion of materials in applications and give examples.

Experiment 22   SPECIFIC HEATS OF METALS

Comments and Hints

    This experiment has been modified in the second edition so as to obtain better results. To make the temperature changes appreciable, a procedure to determine the appropriate T_w has been added. Without this, students may find it frustrating to get only small changes with certain metals and poor results. You may wish to further refine the experiment by computing and suggesting particular amounts of water to be used in the calorimeter cup.

    Although thermal equilibrium is obtained more quickly with metal shot, the author prefers using metal slugs. Slugs eliminate splashing with shot transfer and possible burns. Also, laboratory clean up is facilitated.

    Some instructors use the technique of inserting a styrofoam cup into the calorimeter cup and eliminating the metal stirrer. Assuming no heat loss to the surroundings and stirring with the thermometer, this eliminates the ΔQ term for the cup and stirrer and simplifies Eq. 22-4.

Answers to Selected Experiment Questions

2. (a)   0.22 cal/g-$^{\circ}$C (1 kcal/10^3 cal)(10^3 g/kg) =

                                    0.22 kcal/kg-$^{\circ}$C

    (b)   0.22 cal/g-$^{\circ}$C = 0.22 kcal/kg-$^{\circ}$C (1 Btu/0.252 kcal) x

          (1 kg/2.2 lb)(1°C/1.8°F) = 0.22 Btu/lb-$^{\circ}$F

3.   The hot water would provide an additional contribution to the ΔQ loss side of the energy equation and the measured value of c_m would be greater to account for this.

4.   High specific heat. Water, which has one of the highest specific heats, is relatively inexpensive.

POST-LAB QUIZ QUESTIONS

Completion

1.   The amount of heat required to raise 1 g of a substance by one degree Celsius is called specific heat .

2.   The heat capacity per unit mass is called the specific heat.

3.   The specific heat of water has a value of one in the metric system because of the definition of the calorie or kilocalorie .

4. The specific heat is determined experimentally by the _methods of mixtures_ .

5. The method of mixtures makes use of the conservation _of energy_ .

6. In addition to the masses of the metal sample and water in the experiment, the mass(es) of the _calorimeter cup (and stirrer)_ must also be taken into account.

7. Aluminum with a specific heat of 0.22 cal/g-$^{\circ}$C requires _less_ heat to raise the temperature by a given temperature interval than an equal mass of water.

8. The _larger or greater_ the specific heat of a substance, the more heat is required to raise the temperature of a unit mass by one degree Celsius.

9. If wet, hot metal were used in the experiment, the measured value of c_m would be _greater_ due to this error.

10. A substance with a specific heat of 0.5 cal/g-$^{\circ}$C in units of kcal/kg-$^{\circ}$C has a value of _0.5_ .

Multiple Choice

1. The amount of heat required to raise the temperature of an object by one degree is its *(a) heat capacity, (b) specific heat, (c) latent heat, (d) metal heat.

2. For equal masses of substances with the following specific heats (cal/g-$^{\circ}$C), which would have the greatest temperature change for a given quantity of added heat? *(a) 0.20, (b) 0.40, (c) 0.60, (d) 0.80.

3. If a lower T_c had been used in the experiment, the measured specific heat for a particular metal would be (a) greater, (b) less, *(c) the same.

4. Given the same T_c and T_h and equal masses, for a metal with a smaller specific heat the final temperature T_f would be (a) higher, *(b) lower, (c) the same.

5. An equivalent specific heat of 1 cal/g-$^{\circ}$C for water is (a) 10 kcal/kg-$^{\circ}$C, (b) 0.10 kcal/kg-$^{\circ}$C, (c) 0.5 Btu/lb-$^{\circ}$F, *(d) 1 Btu/lb-$^{\circ}$F.

Essay

1. Discuss in terms of specific heat why we often burn our mouths on some foods, for example, baked potatoes and cheese on a pizza.

2. What considerations should be given to practical applications of storing heat, for example in solar heating applications.

Experiment 23   HEATS OF FUSION AND VAPORIZATION

(Optional: Calibration of a Thermometer)

Comments and Hints

The latent heat experiment can be done in a relatively short time, particularly if the students have had experience with the method of mixtures in Experiment 22.   An optional addendum for the Calibration of a Thermometer has been included for your use if you wish.   It is instructive and conveniently done.

In the latent heat procedures, to get relatively good experimental results for the latent heat of vaporization, it is important to use an in-line water trap to prevent condensed hot water from getting into the calorimeter cup. Glass water traps, such as illustrated in Fig. 23-2, are commercially available.   However, in lieu of these, water traps may be made using Erlenmeyer flasks and two-hole rubber stoppers.   Use glass tubing for the input and output tubes, with the input tube extending well into the flask and the output tube terminating just below the rubber stopper.

Answers to Selected Experiment Questions

2. On the cooler skin, steam condenses and gives up latent heat which causes more serious burns.

3. With the evaporization of perspiration (phase change from liquid to gas), latent heat is taken from the body, thereby causing cooling.   Increased air flow, e.g., from a fan, promotes evaporization and cooling.

5. Either all the ice melts or it doesn't.   If all the ice melts, this requires $\Delta Q = mL_f = (30)(80) = 2400$ cal.

To lower 100 ml or 100 grams of water to 0^oC requires $\Delta Q = mc\ \Delta T = (100)(1)(20) = 2000$ cal, so all of the ice doesn't melt and the final equilibrium temperature is 0^oC with an unmelted mass of ice of $m = \Delta Q/\Delta L = 400/80 = 5$ grams, since 400 cal are not needed to lower the water temperature to 0^oC.

Post-LAB QUIZ QUESTIONS

Completion

1. The energy required to change a unit mass of a solid substance to a liquid is the   (latent) heat of fusion.

2. When a gas condenses to a liquid, the energy released per unit mass is called the (latent) heat of vaporization.

3. The term latent in latent heat descriptively means hidden or concealed .

4. The slope of the graph of Q versus T of a substance for a particular phase is equal to the heat capacity of that phase.

5. At the point of a phase change on a Q versus T graph, the slope has a value of infinity .

6. In the experiment, the latent heats are determined by the method of mixtures .

7. Ice cools a drink by taking latent heat primarily from the drink .

8. Because some heat is lost from the calorimeter in the latent heat of fusion procedure, the final temperature is lower .

9. Because some heat is lost from the calorimeter in the latent heat of vaporization procedure, the final temperature is lower .

10. A change of phase directly from solid to gas is called sublimation .

Multiple Choice

1. The energy associated with a phase change is called (a) heat capacity, (b) specific heat, *(c) latent heat, (d) phase heat.

2. The heat of vaporization of water is (a) 80 cal/g, (b) 100 cal/g, (c) 450 cal/g, *(d) 540 cal/g.

3. If wet ice were used in the experiment, the measured latent heat would be (a) greater, *(b) smaller, (c) the same.

4. If condensed hot water were allowed to enter the calorimeter cup in the heat of vaporization procedure of the experiment, the measured latent heat would be (a) greater, *(b) smaller, (c) the same.

5. The heat released from the condensation of one gram of steam would melt approximately how many grams of ice at $0^{\circ}C$? (a) 1, (b) 3 *(c) 7, (d) 10

Essay

1. Discuss what effects the heats of fusion and vaporization of water would have on the atmospheric temperature.

2. Discuss why the heat of vaporization of a substance is generally larger than the heat of fusion.

Experiment 24   NEWTON'S LAW OF COOLING:
                 THE TIME CONSTANT OF A THERMOMETER

Comments and Hints

    This experiment, with a somewhat novel exponential
decay mechanism, is a good introduction to exponential functions
that will be experienced in later RC circuits and radioactive
decay experiments.   An in-depth treatment of exponential
functions is given in Experiment 52, which involves the
use of semilog and log graph paper.   Some instructors choose
to do Experiment 52 early so students can use these special
graphs.

    Chief experimental considerations for good results
are to make certain that the heating cylinder is far removed
from the cooling thermometer and that there is as little
air disturbance in the vicinity of the cooling thermometer
as possible so as to minimize accelerated convectional
heat loss.

Answers to Selected Experiment Questions

2.   A larger diameter would give more stem surface area
      for cooling and a faster rate.   This would be reflected
      in a larger K, and hence a smaller time constant,
      $\tau = mc/K$.   However, additional mass would increase
      the time constant, so there would be a balancing effect
      in this case.

3.   With a different metal and specific heat c, the time
      constant $\tau = mc/K$ would change accordingly.

5.   (a) For $T = T_r$, then $e^{-t/\tau} = 0$, and t approaches infinity,

      (b) $(T - T_r)/(T_o - T_r) = e^{-t/\tau} = 0.01$, and taking the
      logarithm of both sides, $-t/\tau = \ln 0.01 = -4.6$, and
      $t = 4.6\tau$.

POST-LAB QUIZ QUESTIONS

Completion

1.   The greater the temperature difference between a hot
      object and its surroundings, the __greater__ the cooling
      rate.

2.   An exponential decay curve has a __negative__ exponent
      in the exponential function.

66

3. Bacteria reproduce at a rate represented by an exponential growth curve and hence the function has a __positive__ exponent.

4. The temperature of a cooling object (following Newton's law of cooling) decreases by 63 percent in __one (the first)__ time constant.

5. The greater the specific heat of an object, the __greater__ the time constant for the cooling process.

6. Since e = 2.71, in the first time constant interval for an exponential growth curve, there is a __271__ percent increase over the original value.

7. The logarithmic function in T is to the base __e__ .

8. An exponential decay curve is said to approach the x-axis __asymtotically__ .

9. According to Newton's law of cooling, the rate of change of the temperature of a body is directly proportional to the __temperature difference__ of the body and its surroundings.

10. A limitation of Newton's law of cooling is that the temperature difference be relatively __small__ .

Multiple Choice

1. The exponent of an exponential decay curve is (a) less than one, (b) greater than one, *(c) less than zero, (d) greater than zero.

2. After one time constant, the temperature of a cooling object is which of the following of its initial temperature? (a) e, *(b) 1/e, (c) about 13 percent, (d) about 67 percent.

3. The time constant depends on (a) specific heat, (b) mass, (c) a constant of proportionality, *(d) all of the preceding.

4. The time constant (a) is inversely proportional to the specific heat, (b) has units of inverse time, (c) is the same for all thermometers, *(d) is directly proportional to the mass of the object.

5. The constant K in the time constant ($\tau = mc/K$) has units of (a) s, *(b) cal/$^{\circ}$C-s, (c) cal-s^2, (d) none (unitless)

6.   A thermometer has "recovered" or its temperature decreases
      to less than one percent of its original value in
      how many time constants? (a) 2, (b) 3, (c) 4,
      *(d) 5

Essay

1.   Discuss the decay and growth rate curves for functions
      with different time constants, and suggest some practical
      applications where large and small time constants may
      be desired.

Experiment 25   ARCHIMEDES' PRINCIPLE:
                BUOYANCY AND SPECIFIC GRAVITY

Comments and Hints

The experiment gives students an understanding of
Archimedes' principle, as well as the concept of specific
gravity.   The latter may not be covered in class, but it
is commonly used in hydrometer measurements and students
should be generally familiar with specific gravity.

In the direct proof procedure of Archimedes' principle,
overflow cans are sometimes not available.   An alternate
method has been added for your convenience should you not
have cans available.

Answers to Selected Experiment Questions

3.   By flooding ballast tanks with sea water, the overall
     density of the sub is increased for diving.   Water
     is pumped out of the tanks for less density and surfacing.
     You may wish to call similar attention to ballast
     used for hot-air balloons.

5.   The weight would be the sum of the components.   The
     gravitational weight of the block is unaffected and
     its weight-force pressure is transmitted to the beaker
     bottom (Pascal's principle).

6.   Assuming the metal to be lead (ρ_{Pb} = 11.3 g/cm^3 = 11.3 x
     10^3 kg/m^3), the volume of 45 kg is

     $$V = m/\rho = (45)/(11.3 \times 10^3) = 4.0 \times 10^{-3} \text{ m}^3$$

     (a)   Since the person no doubt lifted the 45 kg in air
           in the first place, this is the mass that could be
           lifted.

     (b)   The mass of an equivalent (displaced) volume of water
           is $m = \rho V$ = (1.0 x 10^3 kg/m^3)(4.0 x 10^{-3} m^3) = 4.0 kg

     Hence, in water the person could lift 45 + 4 = 49
     kg with the help of the buoyant force.

69

POST-LAB QUIZ QUESTIONS

Completion

1. The magnitude of the buoyant force is given by __Archimedes'__ principle.

2. An object will sink in a fluid if the object's density is __greater__ than that of the fluid.

3. An object will remain at the particular level it is placed in a fluid if the density of the object is __the same__ as that of the fluid.

4. A helium balloon rises or "floats" in air because the density of helium is __less than the density of air__.

5. Specific gravity is related to the density of __water__.

6. By the definition of specific gravity, water has a sp. gr. of __1.0__.

7. The unit of specific gravity is __none (unitless)__.

8. The specific gravity of a substance is equal to the magnitude of its density in units of __g/cm^3__.

9. If one cubic object floats higher in water than another with the same size, the higher-floating object is __less__ dense.

10. An instrument used to directly measure the specific gravities of liquids is the __hydrometer__.

Multiple Choice

1. The buoyant force is equal to (a) the density of the fluid, (b) the density of the object, (c) the volume of the object, *(d) the weight of the volume of fluid displaced.

2. An object will float in a fluid if the fluid's density is (a) less, *(b) greater, (c) equal to its own specific gravity, (d) less than one.

3. The comparison standard for specific gravity is (a) air, *(b) water, (c) buoyant force, (d) lead.

4. When a heavy object is submerged in a fluid, the buoyant force is equal to (a) the density of the object, (b) the density of the fluid, (c) the weight of the object, *(d) the weight of the fluid displaced.

5. A liquid with a specific gravity of 4.0 (a) is one-fourth less dense than water, (b) will float on water (if immiscible), *(c) will float an object four times more dense than water, (d) is not possible.

Essay

1. Discuss how specific gravity measurements are used to determine the "strengths" of auto battery acid and antifreeze.

Experiment 26   FIELDS AND EQUIPOTENTIALS

Comments and Hints

In this second edition, the experiment on fields has
been expanded to include magnetic fields, as well as electric
fields.   The purpose is to expand student understanding
of the concepts of a (force) field and equipotentials.
The magnetic field mapping with a compass and iron filings
show the similarity with the electric field, and the various
configurations also show similarities, i.e., dipole fields
and relatively uniform fields between parallel plates and
the poles of a horseshoe magnet.

There are also similarities in equipotentials.   Of
course, the equipotential "lines" for the magnetic fields
are specific for a magnetic pole rather than a moving electric
charge for which the whole plane is an equipotential.
Even so, the idea of no work being done on a charge or
a magnetic pole moving along an equipotential should be
reinforced.

Answers to Selected Experiment Questions

1.   Field lines represent forces and hence have directions.
      Equipotential lines represent paths of equal potential
      or zero work and have no associated direction.

2.   Similarities should be noticed between the field configu-
      rations of (a) an electric dipole and a magnetic N-
      S "dipole", and (b) the parallel plate and the region
      between the poles of the horseshoe magnet (relatively
      uniform).   Also, similarities would be expected for
      two like charges and two like poles.

POST-LAB QUIZ QUESTIONS

Completion

1.   By convention, the electric field at a point is defined
      using a positive (test) charge .

2.   The unit of electric field is   N/C (newton/coulomb).

3.   The direction of the electric field is   toward   a
      negative electric charge.

4.   The closer together the electric field lines, the
       greater the magnitude of the field in that region.

5. Electric potential difference between two points is defined as the <u>work per unit charge (W/q_o)</u> .

6. Paths perpendicular to electric field lines are called <u>equipotentials</u> .

7. Moving a charge along an equipotential requires no <u>work</u> .

8. The magnetic field B is the magnetic force per <u>moving charge</u> .

9. The work done by the magnetic force on a moving charged particle is <u>zero</u> .

10. The electric field of a dipole and the magnetic field between two <u>unlike</u> poles have similar configurations.

Multiple Choice

1. The electric field is (a) a long an equipotential, (b) the same as a magnetic field, (c) the potential difference per charge, *(d) the force per charge.

2. An electric field line ends on a (a) equipotential, (b) north magnetic pole, *(c) negative charge, (d) point in free space.

3. Joule per coulomb (J/C) is the unit of (a) electric field, *(b) potential difference, (c) magnetic intensity, (d) magnetic induction.

4. When an electric charge moves along a field line, *(a) it moves through a potential difference, (b) no work is done, (c) it follows an equipotential, (d) a positive charge is always approached.

5. The SI unit of the magnetic field is the tesla (T), which, from the defining equation $F = qv \times B$, can be seen to be equivalent to (a) N/C, (b) J/C, (c) N-m/C, *(d) N-s/C-m.

6. The magnetic field defined by the force on a moving charge is in the direction of (a) the field, (b) charge motion, *(c) the force experienced by a north magnetic pole, (d) 90° to the force experienced by a magnetic pole.

Essay

1. Discuss the concept of a field, and distinguish between and give examples of scalar and vector fields.

Experiment 27 OHM'S LAW

Comments and Hints

The experiment is straight forward, but for many students it is the first time they have assembled an electric circuit and there is usually some initial difficulty and unfamiliarity with the circuit components.

Probably the most common error is in connecting the rheostat, which commonly has three binding posts. Students often connect the binding post set that gives either a fixed maximum resistance or no resistance. It has been found that an explanation of current flow or tracing through the rheostat proves helpful. Another problem sometimes experienced with a rheostat in the experiment is poor contact between the slide contacts and the resistance wires. Pressing on the contacts usually takes care of it.

As in all electrical experiments, and particularly for initial ones, electrical safety should be stressed.

Answers to Selected Experiment Questions

1. In general, the resistance increases with temperature, so the measured values of current would be less.

2. $V_t = I(R_h + R_s)$, and $R_h = (V_t - R_s)/I$ and $V_h = IR_h$.

POST-LAB QUIZ QUESTIONS

Completion

1. For an ohmic material, the ratio of the voltage and current is equal to __a constant (resistance)__.

2. For a battery circuit, the greater the resistance, the __less__ the current flow.

3. The slope of a V versus I graph is equal to __R (resistance)__.

4. In a liquid circuit analogy, a battery corresponds to a __pump__.

5. Any component in a circuit that does not __generate or supply__ a voltage acts as a resistance.

6. The voltage difference across a resistance is a voltage __decrease or "drop"__.

Exp. 27

7. A voltmeter is connected in __parallel__ with a circuit component to measure voltage.

8. In a circuit with a constant voltage source, the voltage across a resistance may be varied by varying __another resistance__.

9. The algebraic sum of the voltages around a closed circuit is equal to __zero__.

10. For an ohmic resistance, the current is a __linear__ function of the applied voltage.

Multiple Choice

1. The unit of resistance is (a) V, *(b) V/A, (c) A-V, (d) 1/Ω.

2. If the resistance is varied in a battery circuit, (a) the voltage varies, (b) the voltage and current vary, *(c) the current varies, (d) the voltage and current are constant.

3. If the voltmeter had been connected in the circuit in series as the ammeter, the ammeter reading would have been (a) unaffected, *(b) less, (c) greater, (d) fluctuating.

4. If the polarity of the battery had been switched in the experiment, (a) the voltage would change, (b) the current would increase, (c) the slope of the V versus I graph would be reversed, *(d) there would be no observed experimental change.

5. An ammeter *(a) has a small resistance, (b) is connected in parallel with a circuit element, (c) would have been used in place of the voltmeter, (d) produces a large voltage drop in the circuit.

Essay

1. Discuss how a V versus I graph might look for a non-ohmic resistance.

2. Would it be possible for a material to have a V versus I graph with a negative slope? Explain.

Experiment 28   THE POTENTIOMETER: EMF AND TERMINAL VOLTAGE

Comments and Hints

The experiment gives students an understanding of the difference between emf and terminal or "operating" voltage of a battery and experience in use of a potentiometer. This is instructive in learning circuit analysis.

Answers to Selected Experiment Questions

3.   With $V = -Ir + \varepsilon$, the Y-axis intercept ($I = 0$) is the emf or "open circuit" potential difference between the battery terminals ($V = \varepsilon$).   The X-axis intercept ($V = 0$) is the condition if the battery terminals were shorted together ($\varepsilon = Ir$) with only the internal resistance r in the circuit (large I).

POST-LAB QUIZ QUESTIONS

Completion

1.   A battery converts chemical energy into electrical energy.

2.   The potential difference between the terminals of a battery when not connected in a circuit is called electromotive force (emf) .

3.   The terminal or "operating" voltage of a battery differs by its emf by Ir (internal voltage drop) .

4.   Measuring the emf of a battery with a potentiometer requires a standard cell .

5.   The adjustable resistance of a potentiometer acts as a voltage divider .

6.   When a potentiometer is balanced or the galvanometer has a zero or null reading, no (zero) current flows through the cell being measured.

7.   On the experimental graph of V versus I, the Y-intercept of the line is the emf of the cell (open circuit condition).

8.   On the experimental graph of V versus I, the x-intercept of the line is $\varepsilon = Ir$ (short circuit condition) .

9.   For a slide-wire potentiometer, the measured resistance is directly proportional to the length of wire .

10.   The emf and terminal voltage of a battery are approximately the same in a circuit with a large resistance or a small current .

Multiple Choice

1.   A potentiometer can be used to measure the emf of a battery because (a) only a small current flows, (b) the internal resistance is negligible, (c) the terminal voltage is accurately measured, *(d) there is no current in the null condition.

2.   Emf is a (a) force, *(b) potential difference, (c) resistance, (d) current.

3.   For an "open circuit" condition for a battery, *(a) Ir = 0, (b) V = Ir, (c) r = o, (d) ε = Vr.

Experiment 29   THE AMMETER AND VOLTMETER:
            METER SENSITIVITY

Comments and Hints

     With the frequent use of ammeters and voltmeters in
electrical experiments, it is important for students to
know the basic operational principles of these instruments.
(It might save you an ammeter or two.) The experiment furthers
the students' grasp of circuit analysis and is an important
introduction for Experiment 30 (The Measurement of Resistance).

Answers to Selected Experiment Questions

2. and 4.   Circuit diagrams are usually available in texts.
            Essentially, a multimeter requires a switching
            from different shunt and multiplier resistors,
            respectively.

5.   By Eq. 29-6 $V = kn(r + R_m)$, and $(r + R_m)/V = 1/kn$.

POST-LAB QUIZ QUESTIONS

Completion

1.   The "heart" of a dc ammeter or a dc voltmeter is a
      galvanometer .

2.   A galvanometer is essentially a   microamp (current)
      meter.

3.   The constant k for an ammeter circuit is called the
      current sensitivity .

4.   To convert a galvanometer to a practical ammeter, a
      shunt resistance is used.

5.   In an ammeter, the shunt resistance is connected in
      parallel with the galvanometer and is a relatively
      small resistance compared to the coil resistance.

6.   The larger the shunt resistance of an ammeter, the
      less (smaller) the full scale current reading.

7.   The dc voltmeter is a high resistance instrument.

8.   The multiplier resistance of a dc voltmeter is connected
      in series with the galvanometer.

9.   The greater the multiplier resistance of a voltmeter,
      the less the sensitivity of the instrument.

78

Exp. 29

10. A voltmeter is connected in __parallel__ with a circuit
     element and an ammeter is connected in __series__ .

Multiple Choice

1. A galvanometer detects small *(a) currents, (b) resistances,
    (c) voltages, (d) sensitivities.

2. The ammeter (a) is normally connected in parallel with
    a circuit element, (b) contains a multiplier resistance,
    *(c) is a low resistance instrument, (d) contains a
    series shunt resistance.

3. The shunt resistance of an ammeter (a) determines
    the coil resistance, (b) is usually in the kilo-ohm
    range, (c) has no effect on the galvanometer current,
    *(d) determines the meter sensitivity.

4. The multiplier resistance of a voltmeter (a) is in
    parallel with the galvanometer, *(b) prevents large
    currents through the galvanometer, (c) is in series
    with a circuit element resistance, (d) is the same
    order of magnitude as the shunt resistance of an ammeter.

5. A dc voltmeter is what type of instrument? (a) low
    resistance, *(b) low current, (c) with multiplier
    resistance and galvanometer in parallel, (d) a simple
    galvanometer.

6. Which of the following connections with a circuit element
    would be most serious? (a) voltmeter in parallel,
    (b) voltmeter in series, (c) ammeter in series, *(d)
    ammeter in parallel.

Essay

1. Discuss the effects if an ammeter were connected in
    parallel and a voltmeter were connected in series with
    a circuit element. (Consider individually and together.)

Experiment 30   THE MEASUREMENT OF RESISTANCE

Comments and Hints

    This experiment furthers student understanding of the dc ammeter and voltmeter (along with Experiment 29), and makes students aware that these electrical instruments are not "independent" of circuit measurements. Circuit analysis is reinforced, along with the introduction of the Wheatstone bridge.

Answers to Selected Experiment Questions

3.   (a) $V = V_R + V_a = I(R + R_a)$, and $R = (V/I) - R_a = R' - R_a$.

    Then, $R = R'\{1 - (R_a/R')\}$

True resistance (R) is smaller than apparent resistance (R').

    (b) $I_R = I - I_v$, and

$$R = V/I_a = V/(I - I_v) = V/[I - (V/R_v)]$$

$$= (V/I)/[1 - (V/I/R_v)] = R'/[1 - (R'/R_v)]$$

$$= R'\frac{1}{1 - (R'/R_v)} \approx R'[1 + (R'/R_v)]$$

True resistance (R) is larger than apparent resistance (R').

POST-LAB QUIZ QUESTIONS

Completion

1.   The ammeter is a __low__ resistance instrument.

2.   The voltmeter is a __high__ resistance instrument.

3.   For the experimental circuit with the voltmeter directly across a resistance, R = V/I is a good approximation if the voltmeter resistance is __much greater__ than the resistance.

Exp. 30

4.   For the experimental circuit with the voltmeter across the ammeter and resistance, R = V/I is a good approximation if the ammeter resistance is __much less__ than the resistance.

5.   For the experimental circuit with the voltmeter directly across a resistance, the measured resistance is __larger__ than the true resistance.

6.   For the experimental circuit with the voltmeter across the ammeter and resistance, the measured resistance is __smaller__ than the true resistance.

7.   The measurement instrument in a Wheatstone bridge is a __galvanometer__.

8.   When a Wheatstone bridge is balanced, no current flows through the __galvanometer (branch)__.

9.   In a null condition for a Wheatstone bridge, the voltage drops across __adjacent parallel__ bridge arms are equal.

10.   In a null condition for a Wheatstone bridge, the voltage drop across the __galvanometer (branch)__ is zero.

Multiple Choice

1.   In the experimental ammeter-voltmeter circuits, the current through the resistanace is the same as that through the *(a) ammeter, (b) voltmeter, (c) galvanometer.

2.   The voltmeter is what type of instrument?   (a) low resistance, (b) null, *(c) low current, (d) in series

3.   The ammeter is what type of instrument?   (a) in parallel, *(b) low resistance, (c) null, (d) large voltage drop.

4.   In a balanced condition for a Wheatstone bridge, (a) there is no current through the bridge, (c) current flows through the galvanometer branch, (c) the voltage drop across the bridge input and output is zero, *(d) the unknown resistance is directly proportional to the standard resistance.

5.   For a slide-wire Wheatstone bridge, the measured resistance is (a) always equal to the standard resistance, (b) equal to one wire length, *(c) proportional to the ratio of the wire lengths, (d) proportional to the sum of the wire lengths.

Essay

1. Discuss the advantage of measuring resistance with a Wheatstone bridge as opposed to the ammeter-voltmeter method. What is necessary for this advantage?

Experiment 31   RESISTIVITY

Answers to Selected Experiment Questions

3. $A_{Al}^2/A_{Cu}^2 = \rho_{Al}/\rho_{Cu}$, or in terms of diameter,

$$d_{Al} = (\rho_{Al}/\rho_{Cu})^{\frac{1}{2}} d_{Cu}$$

$$= (2.8 \times 10^{-6}/1.72 \times 10^{-6})^{\frac{1}{2}} (0.145) = 0.18 \text{ cm}$$

or No. 13 AWG gauge aluminum wire.

POST-LAB QUIZ QUESTIONS

Completion

1.   The material property of resistance is characterized _resistivity_ .

2.   The resistance of a wire conductor ___increases___ with length.

3.   The resistance of a wire conductor ___decreases___ with greater cross-sectional area.

4.   The diameter of wires increase with ___decreasing___ AWG gauge numbers.

5.   The resistance per length of wires of a given material ___increases___ with increasing AWG gauge numbers.

Multiple Choice

1.   The resistivity is (a) unitless, *(b) independent of the shape of the conductor, (c) proportional to the length of the conductor, (d) inversely proportional to the resistance.

2.   The resistance of a wire conductor (a) increases with cross-sectional area, (b) is independent of shape, *(c) increases with length, (d) is independent of temperature.

3.   If the diameter and length of a wire are doubled, the resistance (a) is the same, *(b) decreases by one-half, (c) doubles, (d) increases by a factor of 4.

83

Experiment 32   THE TEMPERATURE DEPENDENCE OF RESISTANCE

Comments and Hints

The experiment serves to remind that the electrical resistance does not increase with temperature for all materials. Although this is commonly the case for metal conductors, there are exceptions. By using a thermistor, a negative temperature coefficient of resistance is demonstrated.

Answers to Selected Experiment Questions

1. $\alpha = 0.00393 \ 1/^{\circ}C \ (1^{\circ}C/1.8^{\circ}F) = 0.00218 \ 1/^{\circ}F$

2. $R_0(1 + \alpha T)_{Cu} = R_0(1 + \alpha T)_{Ag}$

      $10(1 + 0.00393 \ T) = 10.1(1 + 0.0038 \ T)$

      $T = 0.1/0.0009 = 111^{\circ}C$

5.   Resistance approaches infinity according to formula.

6. $R = R_a(1 - \alpha \Delta T) = R_a \exp \beta(1/T - 1/T_a)$.   Solve for α .

POST-LAB QUIZ QUESTIONS

Completion

1.   The temperature coefficient of resistance has the unit of $1/^{\circ}C.$

2.   To an approximation, the resistance of a metal conductor varies linearly with temperature.

3.   Metals generally have positive temperature coefficients of resistance.

4.   Some materials such as carbon have negative temperature coefficients of resistance.

5.   A negative temperature coefficient of resistance indicates that resistance decreases with increasing temperature.

6.   The unit of the exponential temperature coefficient is the kelvin .

7.   A thermistor is made of a semiconducting material.

Multiple Choice

1.   The fractional change in resistance per unit temperature
      change is called (a) ambient resistance, *(b) temperature
      coefficient of resistance, (c) an exponential function,
      (d) thermistor.

2.   The temperature coefficient of resistance (a) is always
      positive, (b) has the unit of 1/K, (c) has the unit
      of $^{\circ}$C, *(d) is independent of temperature.

3.   In a battery circuit with several carbon resistors,
      one would expect (a) the resistance to remain constant,
      (b) the current to remain constant, (c) the resistance
      to increase slightly with time, *(d) the current to
      increase slightly with time.

Experiment 33 RESISTANCES IN SERIES AND PARALLEL

Comments and Hints

The experimental procedure typifies the scientific method. Students are asked to analyze each circuit theoretically and the computed theoretical predictions are then checked experimentally. You may wish to add more complicated series-parallel circuits for analysis.

Answers to Selected Experiment Questions

2.   (a) All go out, (b) R_2 and R_3 remain lit, (c) R_2 remains lit, (d) all go out, (e) R_1 and R_2 remain lit.

4.   This is a good exercise to get students to think and to give practice at resistances in series and parallel. With four resistances, I get a total of 82 possible resistances (assuming that some combinations do not happen to give exactly the same resistance of a single resistance or another combination). Hopefully not forgetting any combinations, here's how I came up with 82 resistances (S and P for series and parallel connections, respectively): 4 (single), 11 (2S,3S,4S), 11 (2P,3P,4P), 12 (1S-2P), 4 (1S-3P), 6 (2S-2P), 3 (2P-2P in S), 4 (3S-1 in P), 3 (2S-2S in P), 12 (2S-1 in P), and 12 (2S-1 in P and 1S).

Should this question require too much time, reduce the number of resistances to three. This greatly reduces the number of combinations. (See Question 3, Experiment 36 involving three capacitors.)

POST-LAB QUIZ QUESTIONS

Completion

1.   The current through resistances in series is ___the same___ through each resistance.

2.   For resistances in series, the sum of the voltage drops across the resistances is equal to ___the voltage (rise) of the source (battery)___ .

3.   The equivalent resistance for resistances in series is equal to ___the sum of the resistances___ .

4.   The voltage drops across resistances in parallel are equal to the ___voltage of the source___ .

5. For resistances in parallel, the voltage drop across each resistance is the same .

6. The equivalent resistance for resistances in parallel is less than   the smallest individual resistance .

7. When the current divides at a parallel junction, the largest current is through the   smallest resistance.

Multiple Choice

1. In a series resistance circuit, (a) the voltage drop across each resistance is the same, *(b) the current through each resistance is the same, (c) the equivalent resistance is less than the smallest resistance, (d) the current divides between the resistances.

2. In a series resistance circuit, (a) the resistances have a common connection, (b) the reciprocal of the sum of the resistances gives the equivalent resistance, *(c) the equivalent resistance is a maximum, (d) the current times any resistance is equal to the voltage of the source.

3. In a parallel resistance circuit, *(a) the voltage drop is the same across all resistances, (b) the current is always the same through each resistance, (c) the equivalent resistance is equal to the sum of the resistances, (d) the current does not depend on the resistances.

4. In a parallel resistance circuit, (a) the resistance is greater than in a series circuit, (b) the current does not divide, (c) the resistances are connected end-to-end, *(d) the equivalent resistance is a minimum.

5. In a series-parallel circuit, the equivalent resistance is greater than for (a) a series circuit, *(b) a parallel circuit, (c) a similar parallel-series circuit, (d) an open circuit.

Experiment 34 MULTILOOP CIRCUITS: KIRCHHOFF'S RULES

Comments and Hints

This is a new experiment in the second edition of the manual that extends circuit analysis to multiloop circuits. Kirchhoff's rules illustrate two basic physical principles: conservation of electric charge and conservation of electrical energy. A good grasp of these rules and principles helps round out student understanding of circuits.

Answers to Selected Experiment Questions

1. (a) With K_3 read on the 10 mA scale (R_a = 22 ohms),

fractional error R_a/R_3 = 22/680 = 0.032

percent error = 3.2%

(c) With I_3 on the 1000 mA scale (R_a = 0.7 ohm),

fractional error R_a/R_3 = 0.7/680 = 0.001

percent error = 0.1%

4. The circuit is similar to Fig. 34-4 with R_1 and R_2 being the internal resistances of the batteries and R_3 the external resistance. Taking $I_1 + I_2 = I_3$ (where I_2 is reversed to that in Fig. 34-4), for the loop equations:

(loop 1) $V_1 - I_1r_1 + I_2r_2 - V_2 = 0$

or $1.5 - (0.5)I_1 + (0.8)I_2 - 1.2 = 0$

(loop 2) $V_2 - I_2r_2 - I_3R = 0$

or $1.2 - (0.8)I_2 - 2I_3 = 0$

Adding these two equations yields:

$(0.5)I_1 + 2I_3 = 1.5$ or $I_1 = 3 - 4I_3$

From the loop 2 equation: $I_2 = 1.5 - 2.5I_3$

Exp. 34

Substituting these equations into $I_1 + I_2 = I_3$, we have $I_3 = 0.6$ A.

Using this value in the two equations, $I_1 = 0.6$ A and $I_2 = 0$.

POST-LAB QUIZ QUESTIONS

Completion

1. A point where the current divides or comes together in a circuit is called a junction .

2. A path connecting two junctions is called a branch.

3. A branch may contain one or more circuit elements (components) .

4. A closed path of two or more branches is called a loop .

5. The junction theorem involves the conservation of (electric) charge .

6. The loop theorem involves the conservation of electrical energy .

7. According to the junction theorem, the summation of the currents is zero at a junction.

8. According to the loop theorem, the summation of the voltages is zero around a loop.

9. In going around a circuit loop, the voltage difference across a battery is taken to be negative when the battery's negative terminal is in the direction of the motion.

10. In going around a circuit loop, the voltage difference across a resistance is taken to be positive when traversed in the direction opposite to the assigned current.

Multiple Choice

1. A point in a circuit where three or more connecting wires are joined together is called a (a) branch, (b) element, *(c) junction, (d) loop.

2. A path between two junctions is called a *(a) branch, (b) element, (c) loop, (d) Kirchhoff's path.

3. The currents in = currents out at a (a) branch, (b) element, (c) loop, *(d) junction.

4. The sum of the voltages is zero (a) at a junction, (b) across any two elements, *(c) around a loop, (d) across a branch.

5. The junction theorem (a) involves the conservation of electrical energy, (b) states that the summation of the voltages is zero, (c) applies to a loop, *(d) is a statement of the conservation of charge.

6. The voltage difference is taken to be negative when traversing *(a) a resistance in the direction of the assigned current, (b) a battery in the direction of the positive terminal, (c) a loop in a clockwise direction, (d) a junction in the assigned current direction.

Essay

1. Discuss the differences in circuit analyses using Ohm's law and Kirchhoff's rules.

Experiment 35 JOULE HEAT

Answers to Selected Experiment Questions

4. $P = V^2/R$ and $P_1/P_2 = R_2/R_1$ for constant V. But,

$R = \rho L/A$ and with $A = \pi d^2/4$, we have $P_1/P_2 = (L_2/L_1)$

$(d_1/d_2)^2$.

Then, $L_2 = 3L_1$ and $d_1 = 0.1024$ cm (No. 18) and $d_2 =$

0.05105 cm

(No. 24), and $P_1/P_2 = (3)(0.1024/0.05105)^2 = 12$, and

$P_1 = 12P_2$.

5. Low resistances for large currents and large I^2R losses
    or joule heat.

POST-LAB QUIZ QUESTIONS

Completion

1. Electrical power is given by the product of the current
    and the voltage .

2. Joule heat is sometimes referred to as I^2R losses.

3. The joule heat is directly proportional to the resistance
    when the current is constant.

4. The joule heat is inversely proportional to the resistance
    when the voltage is constant.

5. Heat and mechanical energy are related by the mechanical
    equivalent of heat .

6. A calorie is over four times larger than a joule.

7. The kWh is a unit of energy .

8. An incandescent bulb is 95 percent efficient. Thus,
    a 100 W bulb dissipates   95 J   of energy each second
    as joule heat.

Multiple Choice

1. Power (a) has units of kWh, *(b) is the time rate of doing work, (c) is work times time, (d) must be mechanical.

2. When the current through a resistance is doubled, the joule heat (a) remains the same, (b) is doubled, (c) is tripled, *(d) increases by a factor of 4.

3. Electrical power is given by (a) IR, (b) IR^2, *(c) V^2/R, (d) I^2V.

4. Two equal resistances are connected in series and then in parallel with the same battery. How does the joule heat of the parallel circuit compare with that of the series circuit? (a) the same, (b) one-half as great, (c) twice as great, *(d) four times as great.

Experiment 36   THE MEASUREMENT OF CAPACITANCE: BRIDGE METHOD

Answers to Selected Experiment Questions

2.   Total capacitance: $C_s = C_1 C_p/(C_1 + C_p) = (1)(1.5)/(1+ 1.5) =$ 0.6 μF.

$$Q = C_s V = (0.6 \times 10^{-6})(12) = 7.2 \times 10^{-6} \text{ C}$$

C_1 has a charge Q and voltage drop $V_1 = Q/C_1 =$

$(7.2 \times 10^{-6})/(1.0 \times 10^{-6}) = 7.2$ V.

Voltage drop across parallel caps is $V_p = V - V_1 =$

12 - 7.2 = 4.8 V,

and

$$Q_2 = C_2 V_p = (0.5 \times 10^{-6})(4.8) = 2.4 \times 10^{-6} \text{ C}$$

$$Q_3 = C_3 V_p = (1.0 \times 10^{-6})(4.8) = 4.8 \times 10^{-6} \text{ C}$$

3. $C_1 = 0.25$μF, $C_2 = 0.5$ μF, $C_3 = 1.0$μF

Single: 3

Series: 4 (0.17, 0.33, 0.20, and 0.14 μF)

Parallel: 4 (0.75, 1.5, 1.25, 1.75 μF)

2P with 1S: 3 (0.21, 0.36, 0.43μF)

2S-1 in P: 3 (1.17, 0.70, 0.58μF)

Total: 17

POST-LAB QUIZ QUESTIONS

Completion

1.   The ratio of charge to voltage is the __capacitance__ .

2.   The unit of coulomb/volt is called a __farad__ .

3. The modern circuit symbol for a capacitor is _____ .

4. In a capacitance bridge circuit, when the bridge is balanced the voltages across the capacitance arms are equal .

5. In a dc capacitor circuit, the current is zero after a short time.

6. In an ac capacitor circuit, there is an effective current.

7. The equivalent capacitance of capacitors in series is always less than any individual capacitance.

8. The equivalent capacitance of capacitors in parallel is always greater than any individual capacitance.

9. The sum of the individual capacitances gives the equivalent capacitance for capacitors in parallel .

10. The sum of the reciprocals of the individual capacitances gives the reciprocal of the equivalent capacitance for capacitors in series .

Multiple Choice

1. Capacitance has the unit of (a) V-m, *(b) C/V, (c) A-C, (d) F/V.

2. Each capacitor has the same charge when capacitors are connected in *(a) series, (b) parallel, (c) series-parallel, (d) any manner.

3. The voltage difference across each capacitor is the same when capacitors are connected in (a) series, *(b) parallel, (c) series-parallel, (d) any manner.

4. When a capacitance bridge is balanced, (a) the voltages across C_1 and R_1 are equal, (b) the currents through C_1 and C_2 are equal, (c) the voltages across C_1 and R_2 are equal, *(d) the currents through C_2 and R_2 are equal.

5. In order to achieve the largest capacitance from several capacitors, they should be connected in (a) series, *(b) parallel, (c) series-parallel, (d) any manner.

Essay

1. Compare the action of a capacitor in dc and ac circuits.

Experiment 37 THE RC TIME CONSTANT

Comments and Hints

The experiment illustrates the RC time constant. To further promote student understanding, you may wish to set up a "blinker" circuit for the students to observe and investigate.

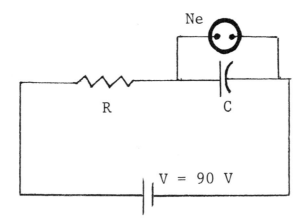

The firing potential of the Ne bulb is about 70 V. As the capacitor charges and the voltage reaches the firing potential, it discharges through the bulb causing it to flash. The charging and the flash rate may be varied by varying R and/or C. Use a variable resistance and/or capacitance with an RC value on the order of a second.

Answers to Selected Experiment Questions

2. $t = 2RC$

   (a) $V = V_o(1 - e^{-2}) = V_o(1 - 0.135) = 0.865\ V_o$

   (b) $V = V_o w^{-2} = 0.135\ V_o$

3. $C = 2 \times 10^{-6} F$, $R = 10^6$ ohms, $V_o = 6$ V, $V/V_o = 0.75$,

   $t = RC = 2.0$ s. Then, with $V/V_o = 1 - e^{-t}/RC$,

   $t = -RC \ln(1 - V/V_o) = -2.0 \ln(1 - 0.75) = -2.0 \ln(0.125)$

   $= 2.8$ s

POST-LAB QUIZ QUESTIONS

Completion

1. A capacitor charges __exponentially__ in a dc circuit.

2. The product RC is called the __time constant__ .

3. The unit of ohm-farad is equivalent to the __second__ .

4. After one time constant, a capacitor has charged to __63__ percent of the maximum voltage.

5. After one time constant, a capacitor has discharged to __37__ percent of its original voltage.

6. An infinite resistance voltmeter measures voltage by means of __electrostatic__ force.

7. For capacitor charging, the slope of $\ln(V - V_o)$ versus t is __$-1/RC$__ .

8. For capacitor discharging, the slope of $\ln(V_o/V)$ versus t is __$1/RC$__ .

Multiple Choice

1. An equivalent unit of second is (a) V/F, (b) F/Ω , *(c) $F\Omega$, (d) V Ω.

2. Given a resistance of 4 $M\Omega$, to have a time constant of one second would require a capacitance of *(a)0.25 μF, (b) 0.50 μF, (c) 2.5 μF, (d) 25 F.

3. An infinite resistance voltmeter (or VTVM) is used in the experiment (a) because this is the only way to measure voltage, (b) to measure ohms instead of volts, (c) because the meter has a time constant similar to the circuit *(d) to prevent capacitor discharge through the voltmeter.

4. If a capacitor in an RC circuit discharges quickly, it (a) is time constant independent, (b) has a large time constant, (c) discharges linearly, *(d) has a small RC.

Experiment 38 INTRODUCTION TO THE OSCILLOSCOPE

Comments and Hints

Most students have never operated an oscilloscope, so it is appropriate to devote a laboratory period to the introduction of this instrument. The chief objectives of the experiment are for students to learn the operation of the various controls and the versatility of the oscilloscope. They generally enjoy turning the knobs and seeing the effects, particularly the Lissajous figures.

Because of the wide variety of oscilloscopes available, it is recommended that the operating manual be furnished. It is a good lesson for students to read the instruction manual of an unfamiliar instrument. Instead of "when all else fails, read the directions", it should be stressed that the directions should be read first and followed so as to avoid damage to an instrument by improper operation.

Answers to Selected Experiment Questions

A2.   The phase angle varies between 0 and 90°. For $\delta = 0$, $x = A \sin 2\pi ft$ and $y = A \sin 2\pi ft$, then $y = x$, which is a straight line with a slope of one and in intercept at the origin ($y = ax + b$).

For $\delta = 90^O$, $x = A \sin 2\pi ft$ and $y = A \cos 2\pi ft$, then

$$x^2 + y^2 = A^2(\sin^2 2\pi ft + \cos^2 2\pi ft) = A^2, \text{ since}$$

$\sin^2 \theta + \cos^2 \theta = 1$, and $x^2 + y^2 = A^2$ is the equation of a

circle with radius A ($x^2 + y^2 = r^2$).

B1. Sweep time = $1/f = 1/60 = 0.017$ s.

B3. See A2 above

POST-LAB QUIZ QUESTIONS

Completion

1.   The basic component of the oscilloscope is a CRT .

2.   The oscilloscope is an extremely fast X-Y plotter.

3.   A sweep rate is generated by a __sawtooth__ wave form.

4.   Stationary wave patterns can be used to measure the wave __frequency__.

5.   Sinusoidal horizontal and vertical inputs give rise to patterns called __lissajous figures__.

6.   Used as an ac voltmeter, __peak-to-peak__ voltages may be measured directly on the oscilloscope screen.

7.   The FOCUS control adjusts the __sharpness__ of the trace.

8.   The vertical sensitivity that adjusts the calibration of volts per grid division is controlled by the __vertical attenuator (or volts/div)__.

9.   To measure the voltage of a signal, the signal is fed into the __horizontal input__.

10. A straight line is obtained when sinusoidal input signals have the same __phase__ and __frequency__.

Multiple Choice

1.   The CR in CRT is (a) a high voltage, *(b) a beam of electrons, (c) a capacitance and a resistance, (d) emitted from the anode.

2.   The sweep time is (a) a vertical function, (b) generated by a sine wave, (c) increases with sweep frequency, *(d) generated by a sawtooth voltage function.

3.   If 3 cycles of a sine wave are observed on the screen with a sweep rate of 100 Hz, then the frequency of the input signal is (a) 100 Hz, (b) 200 Hz, *(c) 300 Hz, (d) 600 Hz.

4.   The amplitude of an input voltage is affected by the (a) intensity, (b) horizontal position, (c) vertical position, *(d) vertical gain.

5.   The general Lissajous figure for signals have in the same frequency but different phases is a (a) straight line, (b) circle, *(c) ellipse, (d) circular loops.

Essay

1.   Explain how stationary displays of sinusoidal input signals are obtained on the oscilloscope display.

Experiment 39   THE RC CIRCUIT OSCILLOSCOPE STUDY

Comments and Hints

    With an introduction to the oscilloscope in Experiment
38, this experiment gives a practical application in the
determination of the time constant of an RC circuit. You
may wish to discuss the discharge decay curve and have the
students examine this part of the display. It is a good
independent exercise to ask for a time constant reading
on the discharge curve.

Answers to Selected Questions

2.   No.   In general, the square wave varies from -V to +V,
     and at the beginning of the cycle as taken in the experi-
     ment Q = C(-V) = -CV.

3.   Knowing R, with the experimental value of t = RC, the
     capacitance C may be calculated.

POST-LAB QUIZ QUESTIONS

Completion

1.   The time constant of an RC circuit is equal to RC .

2.   In one time constant a capacitor charges to 63 percent
     of its maximum voltage amplitude.

3.   For a dc voltage source, the capacitor charges to V_o and
     maintains this voltage unless discharged .

4.   For an ac voltage, the capacitor alternately charges and
     discharges .

5.   In an ac RC circuit, the capacitor charging and discharge
     curves are exponential functions.

6.   The voltage of a capacitor discharging decreases according
     to the function $e^{-t/RC}$.

7.   A capacitor in an RC circuit charges more quickly the
      smaller the time constant.

8.   By increasing the resistance, the capacitor in an RC cir-
     cuit charges more slowly .

Multiple Choice

1. In the experiment the resistance and capacitance (a) are connected in parallel, (b) determine the maximum voltage, *(c) determine the charging rate of the capacitor, (d) give a time constant of R/C.

2. The oscilloscope display is a graph of (a) R vs. C, (b) C vs. t, (c) V vs. C, *(d) V vs. t.

3. If the oscilloscope were connected across the resistance instead of the capacitor, the observed trace would have the form of *(a) a square wave, (b) a sine wave, (c) an exponential curve, (d) a straight line.

Essay-Problems

1. What is percentage of maximum charge on a capacitor in two time constants?

3. What is the percentage decrease of maximum charge for a discharging capacitor (a) in one time constant and (b) in two time constants?

Experiment 40   PHASE MEASUREMENTS AND RESONANCE IN AC CIRCUITS

Comments and Hints

The experiment tests the students' knowledge of ac applications as well as proficiency of oscilloscope operation. An "anti-resonance" circuit and exercise has been added to the experiment in this second edition.

Answers to Selected Experiment Questions

1. (a) $x = A \sin 2\pi ft$ and $y = A \sin (2\pi ft - 90^\circ) = A \cos 2\pi ft$.

Then, $x^2 + y^2 = A^2 (\sin^2 2\pi ft + \cos^2 2\pi ft) = A^2$, which is

the equation of a circle $(x^2 + y^2 = r^2)$.

(b) $x = \sin 2\pi ft$ and $y = A \sin 2\pi ft$, so $x = y$, which is

the equation of a straight line with a slope of one and an intercept at the origin $(y = ax + b)$.

2. (a) Counterclockwise for an inductive circuit $(X_L > X_C)$ and

$\tan \phi = (X_L - X_C)/R > 0$, so ϕ is positive, and voltage leads and current lags.

Clockwise for a capacitive circuit $(X_C > K_L)$, and

$\tan \phi < 0$, etc.

(b) $f > f_r$, the $X_L > X_C$; and $f < f_r$, then $X_C > X_L$.

POST-LAB QUIZ QUESTIONS

Completion

1. The $2\pi ft$ in $\sin 2\pi ft$ is called the _phase angle_ .

2. Common ac voltage varies _sinusoidally_ with time.

3. When the phase constant or difference is positive, the voltage _leads_ the current.

4. The current lags the voltage when the phase constant is _positive_ .

5. When the phase constant or difference is negative, the voltage lags the current.

6. The current leads the voltage when the phase constant is negative .

7. The phase constant is positive when the inductive reactance is greater than the capacitive reactance.

8. When the inductive and capacitive reactances of an RLC circuit are equal, the circuit is in resonance.

9. When driven at its resonance frequency, the impedance of an RLC circuit is resistive (equal to R) .

10. The unit of impedance is the ohm .

Multiple Choice

1. The quantity ϕ is called the (a) phase angle, (b) resonance frequency, (c) impedance, *(d) phase constant.

2. The capacitive reactance (a) has units of farad, *(b) is inversely proportional to the frequency, (c) is directly proportional to the capacitance, (d) always equals the inductive reactance.

3. The impedance of an RLC circuit (a) involves only reactances, (b) is always greater than R, *(c) is frequency dependent, (d) is maximum at resonance.

4. The arctangent of the phase angle of an RLC circuit *(a) depends on the reactance difference, (b) is frequency independent, (c) is equal to one at resonance, (d) increases as the resistance increases.

5. When the phase constant is positive, the *(a) voltage leads, (b) current leads, (c) $X_C > X_L$, (d) circuit is in resonance.

6. When $X_L > X_C$, the (a) current lags, (b) voltage leads, (c) circuit is capacitive, *(d) phase constant is positive.

7. A resonance condition for an RLC circuit is that (a) the phase constant is 90°, *(b) the current in the circuit is maximum, (c) the circuit is capacitive, (d) the phase constant is negative.

Exp. 40

Essay

1. Explain the meaning of the phrase ELI the ICE man.

2. Discuss the significance of resonance in an RLC circuit and how it may be achieved.

Experiment 41   ELECTROMAGNETIC INDUCTION

Comments and Hints

This experiment demonstrates the principle of electro-magnetic induction with the use of simple cylindrical coils. The experiment may be expanded to include transformers at the instructor's option with the use of commercially-available dissectable transformers.

Answer to Selected Experiment Question

2.   Generator principle. Consider the plane of the loop to be parallel to the magnetic field. As the loop rotates through this position, the flux is a minimum, but the <u>change</u> of flux and the induced current are maxima.

Similarly, when the plane of the loop passes through the position it is perpendicular to the field, the flux is a maximum, but the <u>change</u> of flux and the induced current are minima.

POST-LAB QUIZ QUESTIONS

Completion

1.   The magnetic field around a straight, current-carrying wire is in the form of <u>(concentric) circles</u>.

2.   Conventional current is in the direction <u>positive</u> charge carriers would flow.

3.   Looking along a straight, current-carrying wire with the conventional current approaching you, the circular sense of the magnetic field is <u>counterclockwise</u>.

4.   Magnetic flux is a measure of the <u>total magnetic field or number of field lines</u> through an area or loop.

5.   Magnetic induction depends on <u>relative</u> motion between a magnetic field and wire loop.

6.   An important factor in electromagnetic induction is the <u>time rate of change</u> of magnetic flux.

Exp. 41

7. The induced voltage in a wire due to a time rate of change of flux is given by <u>Faraday's law of induction</u>.

8. The direction of an induced current is given by <u>Lenz's law</u>.

9. An induced current is in such a direction that its effects <u>oppose</u> the change that produces it.

10. A change of flux or an induced voltage may be effected with a constant magnetic field by a time rate of change of the <u>area</u> of a wire loop.

Multiple Choice

1. The magnetic flux is (a) given by a right-hand rule, *(b) $B \cdot A$, (c) $\Delta B/\Delta t$, (c) NI.

2. If the magnetic field is constant through a stationary wire loop, (a) the flux is always zero, (b) there is an induced current in the wire, *(c) there is no induced voltage per Faraday's law, (d) Faraday's law does not apply.

3. A time rate of change of flux is given by (a) a right-hand rule, (b) $B \cdot A$, (c) $\Delta B/\Delta A$, *(d) $B(\Delta A/\Delta t)$.

4. Lenz's law (a) is the same as the right-hand rule, *(b) gives the direction of the induced current, (c) is expressed in Faraday's law by a plus sign, (d) gives the permeability of a material.

Essay

1. Discuss Lenz's law, its effects, and what a violation of this law would mean.

105

Experiment 42   RECTIFICATION: SEMICONDUCTOR DIODES

Comments and Hints

This is a very instructive experiment in rectification. Also, it is relatively inexpensive with oscilloscope and sine-wave generator being generally available. Forward and reverse biasing are clearly demonstrated. In this second edition, a filtering circuit and exercise has been added to further student understanding of dc voltage.

This experiment, along with Experiment 43, Transistor Characteristics, provides a good introduction to basic solid state components.

Answers to Selected Experiment Questions

2. As a load or voltage drop.

3. Connect C' in parallel with L' and R. The inductor presents a low impedance to low frequency components ($X_L = 2\pi fL$) and the low frequency components pass to the load. The capacitor presents a low impedance to high frequency components ($X_C = 1/2\pi fC$), and these components take the capacitor path to ground.

POST-LAB QUIZ QUESTIONS

Completion

1. Poor crystalline conductors may be made semiconducting by doping .

2. The charge carriers in N-type semiconductors are electrons .

3. A semiconducting diode is formed by a P-N junction.

4. When a voltage is applied to a diode so as to increase the junction barrier, the diode is said to have reverse bias .

5. A diode conducts when biased in the forward direction .

6. One diode may be used to produce half-wave rectification.

7. A diode is in the OFF mode when reverse biased .

8. When two diodes are connected in opposite directions and in series, the voltage is zero .

9.   A bridge diode circuit may be used to produce <u>full-wave</u>
     <u>rectification</u> .

10. A semi-steady dc voltage may be obtained by <u>filtering</u> .

Multiple Choice

1.   A P-type semiconductor *(a) has impurity atoms with
     fewer valence electrons than the atoms of the host
     material, (b) has electron charge carriers, (c) has
     no doping, (d) is not necessary for a diode.

2.   A P-N diode (a) conducts when reverse biased, (b) junction
     barrier increases when biased in the forward direction,
     *(c) has a conventional current direction from P to
     N, (d) may be used for filtering.

3.   A single diode can be used for (a) filtering, (b) full-
     wave rectification, *(c) half-wave rectification,
     (d) dc to ac conversion.

4.   Filtering allows (a) half-wave rectification, (b) reverse
     biasing, (c) full-wave rectification, *(d) rectified
     ac voltage to approach steady dc voltage.

5.   In the filter circuit in the experiment, the high frequency
     component (a) passed through the load, *(b) was shunted
     to ground through the capacitor, (c) was not passed
     by the diode, (d) is not filtered.

Essay

1.   Distinguish between ac and dc voltages.   Can each be
     converted to the other by means of diodes?

2.   Discuss the purpose of filtering and the impedance
     presented by inductors and capacitors.

3.   Design and explain an hi-pass filter.

Experiment 43   TRANSISTOR CHARACTERISTICS

Comments and Hints

     This new experiment in the second edition of the manual
is designed to give students an introduction to the transistor.
Coupled with Experiment 42 on the semiconductor diode, a
basic understanding of simple solid state components is
obtained in two relatively inexpensive experiments.

     Although perhaps a bit out-of-date, a preliminary,
historical discussion of the vacuum tube and its principles
often helps students understand the operation of a transistor
by analogy.

(The Experiment Questions refer to and are answered from
experimental data.)

POST-LAB QUIZ QUESTIONS

Completion

1.   A semiconductor diode dissipates very little power .

2.   The common middle region of a transistor is called the
      base .

3.   For an NPN transistor, the emitter is N-type semicon-
     ductor.

4.   When normally biased, the emitter-base of an NPN transistor
     is forward biased.

5.   In normal biasing, the collector-base of an NPN transistor
     is reverse biased.

6.   To prevent recombination in an NPN transistor, the base is
      lightly doped.

7.   The current gain in a normally biased NPN transistor
     involves an amplification of the current from the base
     to the collector .

8.   The voltage gain is even greater than the current gain for
     an NPN transistor when the collector-base diode is
      reverse biased.

9. In the characteristic curves for a given base current, as the voltage increases after the transistor becomes conducting, the collector current <u>remains constant</u>.

10. The current gain is given by the ratio $\underline{I_c/I_b}$.

Multiple Choice

1. When a diode is forward biased, (a) V < 0, (b) no current flows, (c) current flows from the emitter to the base, *(d) the direction of the conventional current is from P to N.

2. For a normally biased NPN transistor, (a) the conventional current is from emitter to base, *(b) the electron flow is toward the collector, (c) the collector-base diode is forward biased, (d) large currents flow for a reverse biased emitter-base diode.

3. If the emitter of a transistor is P-type material, then (a) electrons from the emitter travel across the emitter-base diode, (b) the collector is N-type material, *(c) the doped base has an excess of electrons, (d) the transistor cannot be used for amplification.

4. For a normally biased NPN transistor and a given collector voltage V_c, as the base current is increased, the collector current (a) decreases, *(b) increases, (c) is constant.

5. For a typical NPN transistor characteristic curves, for base currents in microamps the collector current is in (a) nanoamps, (b) microamps, *(c) milliamps, (d) amps.

Essay

1. Explain what is meant by amplification. How is this related to gain?

2. How does the operation of a PNP transistor differ from an NPN transistor? (Discuss charge carriers and normal biasing.)

Experiment 44   REFLECTION AND REFRACTION

Comments and Hints

You might say that this experiment is neat as a pin.
With simple equipment (including several pins), double images,
the law of reflection, and Snell's law are demonstrated.
Also, the deflection angle of a rotated mirror is measured.
Some instructors choose to omit this mirror procedure.
It is instructive, particularly with the geometric proof
as an Experiment Question. However, the length of the labora-
tory period and student ability may lend to its exclusion.

Answers to Selected Experiment Questions

1. (b) During the day, the incoming light masks the reflected
internal light.

3. The hand is held over the image of a candle seen in
the glass window. The candle (not shown) is in front
of the window.

4. Referring to the figure,

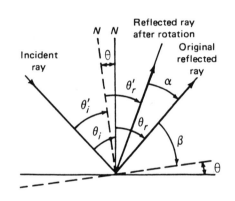

$$\theta_r + \beta + \theta = \theta_r' + \alpha + \beta$$

and $\alpha = \theta + \theta_r - \theta_r'$

But, $\theta_i - \theta_i' = \theta = \theta_r - \theta_r'$

so $\alpha = 2\theta$

5. Calling the incident angle of the RC' ray in the glass θ_3
and the refracted angle of the ray C'C" in air θ_4, by
Snell's law, $n_a \sin \theta_1 = n_g \sin \theta_2$ and $n_g \sin \theta_3 = n_a$
$\sin \theta_4$, where n_a and n_g are the indices of refraction of
air and glass, respectively. From the internal ray RC', it
should be evident that $\theta_2 = \theta_3$, and $n_a \sin \theta_1 = n_a \sin \theta_4$,
so $\theta_1 = \theta_4$.

Hence, the incident and emergent rays (CR and C'C") are
parallel.

Exp. 44

By trigonometry, the lateral displacement d is $d = y \tan \theta_2$, where y is the thickness of the plate.

POST-LAB QUIZ QUESTIONS

Completion

1. In symbol form, the law of reflection is expressed as $\underline{\theta_i = \theta_r}$.

2. The reflection from a mirror surface is called <u>regular (specular)</u> reflection.

3. The reflection from this page is called <u>irregular (diffuse)</u> reflection.

4. For a plane mirror, the image distance and object distance are <u>equal</u> .

5. The angles of reflected rays and refracted rays are measured relative to a <u>line perpendicular (normal)</u> to the surface.

6. When a light ray enters another medium, the ray is generally <u>refracted</u> .

7. When a light ray enters an optically less dense medium, it is bent <u>away</u> from the normal.

8. The (absolute) index of refraction is equal to the ratio of <u>c/v</u> .

9. Given the index of refraction of a material and the incident angle of a light ray, the angle of refraction may be computed from <u>Snell's law</u> .

10. The speed of light in a material may be computed if the <u>index of refraction</u> of the material is known.

11. The index of refraction of a material or substance is always <u>greater</u> than one, with the index of refraction of <u>vacuum</u> being equal to one.

12. When a mirror is rotated by an angle θ , a light ray is deflected by an angle of <u>2θ</u> .

Multiple Choice

1. The reflection of mirror surface is called (a) diffuse reflection *(b) specular reflection, (c) irregular reflection, (d) dependent on the index of refraction.

2. The angle of reflection is equal to the (a) angle of refraction, (b) $\sin \theta_1$, (c) lateral displacement, *(d) angle of incidence.

3. The ratio of the velocities of light in two media is called the (a) law of reflection, (b) refraction angle, *(c) relative index of refraction, (d) absolute index of refraction.

4. The relative index of refraction *(a) may be greater than, equal to, or less than one, (b) is always greater than one, (c) is always equal to one, (d) is always less than one.

5. For a light ray entering a more optically dense medium, (a) $\theta_2 = \theta_1$, *(b) $\sin \theta_2$ is less than $\sin \theta_1$, (c) the ray is reflected, (d) the (absolute) index of refraction is less than one.

Essay

1. Discuss the different types of reflection. Does the law of reflection apply in all cases? Explain.

2. Distinguish between the relative and absolute indices of refraction.

3. Discuss the case of a light ray going from an optically denser medium to an optically less dense medium in terms of relative magnitudes of incident and refraction angles and Snell's law.

Experiment 45   SPHERICAL MIRRORS AND LENSES

Comments and Hints

    This experiment provides students a basic understanding
of the theoretical principles of spherical mirrors and lenses
learned in class.   Students generally have difficulty in
"visualizing" the formation of images.   In the experimental
procedures, students are asked to first sketch a ray diagram
for a particular case.   With this knowledge, the case is
investigated experimentally, and the experimental results
compared with computed values.   The observation of real
images facinates and excites students.   They also learn
that diverging mirrors and lenses do not form real images.

    Note: If candles are used in the experiment, students
should be cautioned about accidentally being burned and
about keeping long hair away from the candle flame.

Answers to Selected Experiment Questions

1.   (a) and (b). $1/d_o + 1/d_i = 1/f = 1/\infty = 0$, and $d_i = -d_o$.

4.   If $d_i = d_o$, then $1/d_o + 1/d_i = 1/d_i + 1/d_i = 2/d_i = 1/f$,

    and $d_i = d_o = 2f$.

POST-LAB QUIZ QUESTIONS

Completion

1.   A concave spherical mirror has the reflecting surface
     on the   __inside__ of a spherical section.

2.   For a spherical mirror, the radius of curvature is
     __twice (2x)__ the focal length.

3.   A diverging spherical mirror has a __convex__ reflecting
     surface.

4.   Light rays parallel to the optic axis of a concave
     spherical mirror converge at __the focal point__ .

5.   An image is magnified if the __image__ distance is greater
     than the __object__ distance.

6.   A positive image distance indicates that the image
     is __real__ .

7. For a spherical lens, the focal length is generally not equal to $R/2$.

8. The focal length of a spherical lens depends on the radii of curvature and the index of refraction .

9. The spherical lens equation applies only to thin lenses.

10. When $d_i = d_o$ for a spherical lens, the focal length is equal to $d_i/2$ or $d_o/2$.

Multiple Choice

1. In ray diagrams for spherical mirrors, which ray goes through or appears to go through the center of curvature? *(a) chief ray, (b) parallel ray, (c) focal ray

2. A converging mirror may form (a) real images only, (b) virtual images only, *(c) real and virtual images, (d) no images at all.

3. An upright image is indicated by a (a) $+f$, (b) $+d_o$, *(c) $-d_i$ (d) $-M$.

4. A virtual image will be formed by a converging lens (a) when $d_o > R$, *(b) when $d_o < f$, (c) when $d_o = d_i$, (d) never.

5. For a symetrical spherical lens to have $f = R/2$ requires (a) $d_i = d_o$, (b) $M = 1$, (c) $d_i = 2f$, *(d) $n = 2$.

Essay

1. Discuss the formation of real and virtual images in terms of light ray energy.

Experiment 46   OPTICAL INSTRUMENTS:
                 THE MICROSCOPE AND THE TELESCOPE

Comments and Hints

The basic principles of the microscope and the telescope provide convenient applications of lenses. The magnifications given by these instruments are applied to the study of minute and astronomical objects. The distinction between astronomical and terrestrial telescopes is particularly instructive in upright and inverted images.

Answers to Selected Experiment Questions

2. Referring to Fig. 46-1, by similar triangles $y_i/\theta_i = y_o/\theta_o$, and m = $y_i/y_o = \theta_i/\theta_o$.

3. Clear images of magnified objects are limited to about 3X magnification because of aberrations, e.g., spherical aberration.

4. A third "erecting" convex lens may be placed between the objective and the eye piece. This lens merely inverts the image without magnification. However, the length of the telescope is increased by four times the focal length of the erecting lens. This method is used in "spy glasses" which are "telescoped" into long lengths. (Recall the old pirate movies.)

POST-LAB QUIZ QUESTIONS

Completion

1. A simple microscope consists of a __converging (convex)__ lens.

2. The magnification of an object viewed through a magnifying glass is given by the __angular (θ_i/θ_o)__ magnification.

3. For magnification, the virtual image of the lens or lenses system is positioned at the __near point__ of the eye.

4. A simple compound microscope consists of __two converging (convex)__ lenses.

5. The objective of a compound microscope produces a _real_ image inside the focal point of the _eyepiece (ocular)_ .

6. The total magnification of a compound microscope is equal to the product of the _lateral_ and _angular_ magnifications.

7. A reflecting telescope uses a _converging (concave)_ mirror and a refracting telescope uses a _converging (convex)_ lens to form the image of a distant object.

8. The image of an astronomical telescope is _inverted_ .

9. A Galilean terrestrial telescope has a _diverging (concave)_ lens as an eyepiece.

10. The magnification of an astronomical telescope is given by the ratio of _f_o/f_e (f of objective/f of eyepiece)_ .

Multiple Choice

1. A simple microscope consists of (a) a lens and a mirror, (b) a mirror, *(c) a single lens, (d) two lenses.

2. A simple compound microscope consists of (a) two mirrors, (b) a mirror and a converging lens, (c) a converging lens and a diverging lens, *(d) two converging lenses.

3. The objective of a compound microscope *(a) has a short focal length, (b) produces a virtual image, (c) is called an ocular, (d) is a diverging lens.

4. An astronomical telescope (a) has no magnification, (b) produces a virtual image, *(c) produces an inverted image, (d) is the same as a Galilean telescope.

5. A terrestrial telescope *(a) may be used for astronomical observations with no problem, (b) has an inverted image, (c) has two converging lenses, (d) can only be used on Earth.

Essay

1. Discuss why the inverted image of an astronomical telescope presents no problem to an astronomer and why larger reflecting telescopes than refracting telescopes can be built.

Experiment 47   POLARIZED LIGHT

Comments and Hints

   Not many lab manuals have a detailed experiment on polarized light.   This is unfortunate, since polarization is a
fascinating subject and "fun" to work with and apply.   So
this problem no longer exists in our manual, this new experiment has been incorporated in the second edition.   It is hoped
that you will find it beneficial.

   A couple of comments regarding cellophane tape used in
the experiment.   One, it must be cellophane tape and not the
now-common polymer variety.   Two, cellophane tape has become
difficult to find in stores.   You may have to order some.

Answers to Selected Experiment Questions

1.   For $\theta_p = 45^\circ$, we have from $\tan \theta_p = n$ that $n = 1$

   ($\tan 45^\circ = 1$), which is the index of refraction of

   vacuum.   Smaller angles would require an index of re

   fraction less than one, which cannot be obtained (for

   the absolute index of refraction, $n = c/v$).

4.   A beam of polarized light could be split, the planes

   of polarization of the components rotated slightly at

   different angles with polarizers and at right angles

   with liquid crystals, then the components could be

   recombined, giving random, unpolarized vector vibra

   tions.   This would be a lot of work.

POST-LAB QUIZ QUESTIONS

Completion

1. Another name for linear polarization is __plane__ polari-
    zation.

2. A substance that has the property of linearly polarizing
    transmitted light is called __dichroic__.

3. The polarization direction of light passing through
    a Polaroid sheet is __perpendicular__ to the orientation
    direction of the molecular chains.

4. The fraction of the intensity of polarized light transmitted
    through an analyzer is given by __$\cos^2\theta$__.

5. The polarization angle for polarization by reflection
    is given by __$\tan\theta_p$__.

6. The transmission axis of the lenses of polarizing sun-
    glasses is oriented __vertically__.

7. An anisotropic crystal with two indices of refraction
    exhibits __double refraction (birefringence)__.

8. The scattering of sunlight by atmospheric gases is
    called __Rayleigh scattering__.

9. A substance that rotates the plane of polarization
    of polarized light is said to exhibit __optical activity__.

10. A liquid in which the molecules have some order is
    termed a __liquid crystal__.

Multiple Choice

1. Polarization by selective absorption depends on the
    property of (a) Brewster's law, *(b) dichroism, (c)
    scattering, (d) optical activity.

2. Brewster's law describes polarization by *(a) reflection,
    (b) refraction, (c) scattering, (d) selective absorption.

3. For the expression $I = I_o \cos^2\theta$, across-polarizers is the
    condition for (a) $\theta = 0^O$, (b) $\theta = 45^O$, (c) $\theta = 60^O$,
    *(d) $\theta = 90^O$.

4. An extraordinary ray is involved in polarization by (a) reflection, *(b) refraction, (c) scattering, (d) selective absorption.

5. Skylight is partially polarized by (a) selective absorption, (b) reflection, (c) refraction, *(d) scattering.

6. To compute the polarization angle for polarization by reflection by a material, one needs to know the (a) optical activity, (b) plane of polarization, *(c) index of refraction, (d) dichroism.

7. LCD's use the property of (a) dichroism, (b) birefringence, (c) double refraction, *(d) optical activity.

8. Optical stress analysis may be done on a material that is *(a) optically anisotropic, (b) dichroic, (c) described by Brewster's law,(d) optically active.

Essay

1. Describe the various ways by which light may be polarized.

2. Explain the operation of an LCD.

3. Can a longitudinal wave be polarized? Explain.

Experiment 48   THE PRISM SPECTROMETER:
                 DISPERSION AND INDEX OF REFRACTION

Comments and Hints

This experiment is basically an introduction to spectrometry. It illustrates dispersion, and the major procedure is to measure the angle of deviation, and hence, the index of refraction for a particular light component. This use of the spectrometer sets the stage for the following experiment (Experiment 49 Line Spectra and the Rydberg Constant) which involves the measurement of spectral lines.

Answers to Selected Experiment Questions

1. Referring to Fig. 48-4, consider a ray incident on the apex of the prism that is split and reflected from the prism sides (only one side need be drawn because of symmetry). Extending a line from the prism side, it should be evident from the drawing that the angle between the telescope settings is

$$Angle = 2a + A$$

where a is the angle between the reflected ray and the side of the prism. Also, $\theta_i + \theta_r + a + A/2 = 180^{\circ}$, and $\theta_i + a = 90^{\circ}$ or $2(\theta_i + a) = 180^{\circ}$. Equating, and using the law of reflection ($\theta_i = \theta_r$), we have $2\theta_i + a + A/2 = 2\theta_i + 2a$, and $a = A/2$. Hence, the angle is 2A.

POST-LAB QUIZ QUESTIONS

Completion

1. Monochromatic light has a single wavelength or color.

2. The wavelength of light in a medium is less (shorter) than the wavelength of the light in vacuum.

3. Dispersion arises because the index of refraction (wave-length) is slightly different for each component of light in a medium.

4. The angle between the original beam direction and an emergent component of the beam is called the angle of deviation .

5. As the angle of incidence is varied, the angle of deviation goes through a __minimum__ .

6. The angle of minimum deviation of a light component and the prism angle are related to the __index of refraction__ for that component.

7. A parallel incident beam is produced by a __collimator__ .

8. The angles involved in a spectroscopic mesurement are measured by means of a __divided circle__ .

9. The dispersed prism light is observed by means of a __telescope__ .

10. If the wavelength of light in vacuum and in a medium were the same, there would be no __dispersion__ .

Multiple Choice

1. For light in vacuum and in a medium (a) the speeds are the same, (b) the wavelengths are the same, *(c) the frequencies are the same, (d) the indices of refraction are the same.

2. The angle of deviation is greatest for *(a) violet light, (b) yellow light, (c) red light, (d) green light.

3. Which one of the following is not a basic part of a spectrometer? (a) a prism, (b) a divided circle, (c) a telescope, *(d) a source.

4. A parallel beam is obtained by means of a (a) telescope, *(b) collimator, (c) prism, (d) dispersion.

5. As the wavelength of light increases, the angle of deviation *(a) decreases, (b) increases, (c) is unchanged.

Experiment 49   LINE SPECTRA AND THE RYDBERG CONSTANT

Comments and Hints

The experiment introduces students to line spectra, which previously have usually had only textbook description and diagrams. The actual "seeing" of line spectra is very instructive.

As pointed out in the experiment, caution should be observed with the high voltage tubes and large mercury sources should be properly shielded for protection from ultraviolet radiation.

Answers to Selected Experiment Questions

1. $R_t = 13.6/hc = (13.6 \text{ eV})/(4.14 \times 10^{-15} \text{ eV-s})(3 \times 10^8 \text{ m/s})$

$= 1.095 \times 10^7 \text{ 1/m} (1 \text{ m}/10^{10} \text{ Å}) = 1.095 \times 10^{-3} \text{ Å}^{-1}$

2.   Wavelengths of lines outside of the visible region.

3.   As $n \to \infty$, the wavelength approaches

$\lambda = 4/R = 4/(1.097 \times 10^7 \text{ 1/m}) = 3.65 \times 10^{-7} \text{ m}$

$= 3.65 \times 10^3 \text{ Å}$

POST-LAB QUIZ QUESTIONS

Completion

1.   The spectrum from an incandescent source is __continuous__.

2.   Light emitted from an excited gas has a __line (discrete)__ spectrum.

3.   A line spectrum is specific for a particular __substance__.

4.   Line spectra are emitted as a result of __electron__ transitions between atomic energy levels.

5.   One angstrom is equal to __10^{-8}__ cm. and __10^{-10}__ m.

6.   The hydrogen spectral lines in the visible region are called the __Balmer__ series.

7.   The Rydberg constant is an __empirical__ constant for hydrogen spectra.

Exp. 49

8. A theoretical explanation of hydrogen line spectra was developed by <u>Niels Bohr</u>.

9. The n's in the Bohr theory are called <u>principal quantum numbers</u>.

10. The final state for the transitions of the Balmer series is <u>n = 2</u>.

Multiple Choice

1. Discrete spectra are observed for (a) all substances, (b) incandescent sources, (c) only hydrogen discharge tubes, *(d) vaporized solids.

2. The most intense spectral line for hydrogen has a wavelength corresponding to (a) green, *(b) red, (c) yellow, (d) violet.

3. The hydrogen series in the infrared region is the *(a) Paschen series, (b) Balmer series, (c) Rydberg series, (d) Lyman series.

4. Transitions between energy levels with smaller spacings produce spectral lines with (a) greater frequencies, (b) lines always in the visible region, *(c) longer wavelengths, (d) a continuous nature.

Essay

1. Discuss the difference between continuous spectra and line spectra.

Experiment 50   THE TRANSMISSION DIFFRACTION GRATING:
                 MEASURING THE WAVELENGTH OF LIGHT

Comments and Hints

Students often (sometimes) wonder how wavelengths of light on the order of 10^{-7} m are measured (or you may want to spark their imaginations by asking). This is a very small length. The experiment answers the question and introduces the diffraction grating.

You have the choice of two experimental methods with the use of a spectrometer or a more inexpensive optical bench. For either method caution should be observed for the high voltage tubes and large mercury sources should be properly shielded to protect against ultraviolet radiation. A sodium source is suggested for the optical bench method because of the distinctive yellow lines.

Answers to Selected Experiment Questions

1. $d \sin \theta_n = n\lambda$ and $d = 1/N$, hence $\sin \theta_n = Nn\lambda$. Thus as N increases so does $\sin \theta_n$, or the angle θ_n.

3.   Yes. For continuous spectrum orders, $d \sin \theta_1 = \lambda_1$ and $d \sin \theta_2 = 2\lambda_2$ for n = 1 and n = 2, respectively, where λ_1 and λ_2 may be different wavelengths. If $\lambda_1 = 2\lambda_2$, then $\theta_1 = \theta_2$ and the orders overlap.

4.   With $d \sin \theta_n = n\lambda$ or $\sin \theta_n = n\lambda/d$, the sine has a maximum of one, so the theoretical limit is $n\lambda/d = 1$ or $n_{max} = d/\lambda$. However, in practice only the first few orders are easily observed. Notice than an n_{max} order would give a $\theta_{max} = 90^{\circ}$.

Exp. 50

POST-LAB QUIZ QUESTIONS

Completion

1. Reflection gratings are ruled on _polished metal_ and
   transmission gratings are ruled on _glass_ .

2. Diffraction refers to the _bending (deviation)_ of waves
   around sharp edges or corners.

3. For a diffraction pattern, complete constructive interference of waves occurs when the phase or path difference
   is equal to _one wavelength_ .

4. The grating constant is the distance between _grating lines_ .

5. The greater the number of grating lines per unit length,
   the _smaller_ the grating constant.

6. The image orders are _symmetric_ on either side of the
   central maximum.

7. For white light, each image order is a _continuous_
   spectrum.

8. The central maximum has an order number of _n = 0_ .

Multiple Choice

1. For a glass diffraction grating, (a) there is no first
   order image, *(b) the unruled slit areas transmit
   light, (c) the patterns are formed by reflected light,
   (d) the grating constant is equal to N.

2. If a particular grating has a greater grating constant
   than another, then (a) it has a greater number of lines
   per unit length, (b) there is no difference in the
   diffraction patterns of each, (c) its diffraction
   pattern will be spread out more, *(d) more orders
   will be practically observed.

3. If a monochromatic source with a greater wavelength
   is used for a diffraction experiment, then *(a) the
   diffraction pattern is spread out more, (b) more orders
   will be practically observed, (c) the patterns are
   the same, (d) the grating constant increases.

Experiment 51 THE MASS OF AN ELECTRON: e/m MEASUREMENT

Comments and Hints

   A common method of measuring the e/m of an electron
involves a special e/m vacuum tube and Helmholtz coils
(Bainbridge method). These setups are expensive and in
general this is restrictive for large introductory physics
labs. The method described in this experiment using a tuning-
eye vacuum tube and air-core solenoid addresses this problem.
Along with commonly available supplementary equipment,
these items provide a relatively inexpensive method for
students to perform an important experiment in modern physics.

Answers to Selected Experiment Questions

2.   The protons would be attracted to the negatively charged
     deflection electrodes and would be repelled by the
     conical anode, so little or nothing would be observed.
     If the polarities for these tube components were
     reversed, a fan-shaped pattern with reverse radii
     of curvature would be observed, but a greater magnetic
     field would be required because of the proton's greater
     mass (1846 times that of the electron). The value of
     e/m would also be much smaller.

3.   Yes. Instead of varying the solenoid current to match the
     radius of curvature to a reference object, the solenoid
     current could be at some appropriate constant value
     for various anode voltages and different reference
     objects could be used to match the observed radii
     of curvature.

POST-LAB QUIZ QUESTIONS

Completion

1.   The determination of the mass of an electron depends on
     knowing the (electron) charge .

2.   The force, in terms of the magnetic field, that supplies
     the centripetal force for the electron moving in a circle
     is equal in magnitude to evB .

3.   The magnetic force on the electron is always at right angles
     (90°) to the electron motion.

4.   (Option, right-hand rule). A uniform magnetic field is
      into the plane of the page of this paper. If an electron
      enters the field traveling across the plane of the paper
      from the bottom of the page, it will be initially de-
      flected toward the right side of the page .

5.   The work done on the electron by the magnetic force is
       zero   (W = F·r = 0) .

6.   Once an electron with a constant velocity enters a magnetic
      field, its speed is constant .

7.   For electrons of a given speed, if the magnetic field is
      increased, their radius of curvature is less (decreased) .

8.   The electrons are attracted toward the anode in the tube.

9.   Without a magnetic field, the observed shadow patterns are
       wedge shaped.

10.   The magnetic field of the solenoid is directly propor-
      tional to the turn density and directly proportional
      to the solenoid current.

Multiple Choice

1.   The unit of the ratio of e/m is (a) A/N, (b) C/lb,
      *(c) C/kg, (d) A/kg.

2.   The magnitude of the ratio of e/m for an electron (e^- =
      1.6×10^{-19} C and m = 9.1×10^{-31} kg) is on the order of
      (a) 10^{-11}, (b) 10^{-15}, (c) 10^{-23}, *(d) 10^{12}.

3.   The initial electron speed is provided by a (a) magnetic
      field, *(b) potential difference, (c) centripetal force,
      (d) solenoid current.

4.   The radius of curvature of the electrons increases with
      (a) increasing magnetic field, *(b) increasing tube poten-
      tial difference, (c) decreasing initial speed, (d) de-
      creasing magnetic force.

Experiment 52   EXPONENTIAL FUNCTIONS

Comments and Hints

There are many exponential or logarithmic processes in physics. In graphically representing exponential functions, they may be converted to straight line graphs on Cartesian graph paper by plotting logarithms. However, it is convenient and time-saving to plot these functions on either semilog or log graph papers.

This experiment is a study of exponential functions and the use of semilog and log graph papers. It is considered important for students to have an introduction to and some familiarization with these graph papers. It is also important for students to know how to convert functions to straight line forms on Cartesian graph paper. The latter was done in various previous experiments, e.g., Experiment 37 on the RC circuit. Exponential functions are placed here in the manual in anticipation of nuclear exponential processes. However, some instructors prefer to introduce these functions earlier.

In either case, the experiment is instructive and inexpensive. A new procedure involving wire gauge numbers and diameters has been added to show the exponential relationship between these quantities.

Answers to Selected Experiment Questions

4. In $t = 1$ year, with a 1% growth rate, $N_O + 0.01N_O = N$,

    or $N/N_O = 1.01 = e^{\lambda t} = e^{\lambda}$, and $\lambda = 0.00995$ (y^{-1}).

    Then, for $N/N_O = 2 = e^{\lambda t}$, we write $\ln 2 = 0.693 = \lambda t$

    and $t = 70$ years.

5. $N/N_O = 0.01 = e^{-t/\tau}$ or $\ln 0.01 = -4.6 = -t/\tau$, and

    $t = 4.6\tau$. With $t_{\frac{1}{2}} = 0.693\tau$, then $t/t_{\frac{1}{2}} = 4.6\tau/0.693\tau$

    $= 6.6$ or after 6.6 half-lives.

Exp. 52

6.   Given $d = d_o e^{-\lambda n}$, then

$$R/L = \rho/A = 4\rho/\pi d^2 = (4\rho/\pi d_o^2)e^{2\lambda n}.$$

Comparing with $R/L = (R_o/L_o)e^{\lambda' n}$ it is seen that $\lambda' = 2\lambda$, or the growth constant is twice the decay constant.

POST-LAB QUIZ QUESTIONS

Completion

1.   In an exponential process, a variable quantity grows or decays at a rate proportional to the quantity's <u>present value</u>.

2.   A decay process has a <u>negative</u> decay constant.

3.   For a time process, the growth or decay constant has units of <u>time</u>$^{-1}$.

4.   An exponential process is also called a <u>logarithmic</u> process.

5.   In one half-life, a quantity decays to <u>one-half of its original value</u>.

6.   The inverse of a growth or decay constant is called the <u>time constant</u>.

7.   In one time constant for a growth process, the variable increases <u>e^1 (2.718)</u> times its original value.

8.   On a Cartesian graph of an exponential decay function, the curve is said to approach the x-axis <u>asymptotically</u>.

9.   To obtain a straight line graph from a function of the form $N = N_o e^{-bt}$ by plotting direct values of N and t, <u>semilog</u> graph paper should be used.

10.   To obtain a straight line graph for a function of the form $y = ax^n$ by plotting direct values of y and x, <u>log (log-log)</u> graph paper should be used.

Multiple Choice

1. A negative time constant indicates a (a) large doubling time, (b) a large growth constant, *(c) a decay process, (d) linear function.

2. The time constant (a) is always positive, (b) has units of time, (c) is equal to twice the half-life, *(d) has units so the exponent is unitless.

3. In one half-life, (a) $N/N_o = 2$, (b) $t = \tau/2$, (c) $N = eN$, *(d) $N_o = 2N$.

4. What fraction of the original value of a quantity is present in an exponential decay process at the end of three half-lives? (a) 1/3, (b) 1/4, *(c) 1/8, (d) 1/9

5. In computing the slope of a straight line on a semilog graph of N versus t, the Δy term is *(a) $\ln N_2/N_1$, (b) $N_2 - N_1$, (c) $t_2 - t_1$, (d) $\ln N/t$.

Essay

1. Discuss the limits or values of exponential growth and decay processes after long times.

2. Analyze the function $N = N_o(1 - e^{-t/\tau})$. That is, is it a decay or growth process? What is the form of its Cartesian graph? What occurs after a long time? etc.

Experiment 53   THE CHART OF NUCLIDES

Comments and Hints

As an introduction to nuclear physics, this experiment on the Chart of Nuclides provides students with a greater understanding and appreciation of isotopes, half-lives, decay processes, etc. For the price of a Chart of Nuclides, it is a bargain.

The nuclide displays in the chart give a great deal more information than is needed for an introductory lab. You may wish to exclude or explain some of the unfamiliar terms or processes to your students, or simply allow them to pick out the items they know or are referred to in the experiment. Also, you may wish to omit certain exercises to shorten the experiment.

Answers to Selected Experiment Questions

14. (a) $^{10}B(n,\alpha)^{7}Li$ ^{11}B (compound nucleus)

     (b) $^{16}O(n,p)^{16}N$ ^{17}O

     (c) $^{7}Li(p, \gamma)^{8}Be$ ^{8}Be

     (d) $^{17}O (\gamma ,np)^{15}N$ ^{17}O

     (e) $^{32}S(n,p)^{32}P$ ^{33}S

     (f) $^{3}H(d,n)^{4}He$ ^{5}He

     (g) $2_{H}(t,n)^{4}He$ ^{5}He

POST-LAB QUIZ QUESTIONS

Completion

1. The chart of nuclides is a graph of <u>Z versus N</u> .

2. A horizontal row in the chart is a family of <u>isotopes</u> .

3. The nuclides in a vertical column in the chart all have the same number of neutrons .

4. The squares of stable nuclides are shaded gray .

5. A nuclide with isomeric states has one or more different radioactive (decay) modes .

6. Nuclear isomers have the same Z and N numbers but different radioactive properties .

7. A nuclide represented by a white square is artifically produced .

8. For a neutron as an "in" particle in a nuclear process, the square of the compound nucleus on the chart is located one square to the right from the original nuclide.

9. For β^+ decay, the square of the daughter nuclide on the charge is located one square diagonally to the lower right from the parent nuclide.

10. For an (α,n) reaction, the square of the product nuclide on the chart is located 2 up and 1 to the right from the original nuclide.

Multiple Choice

1. Isotones on the chart are in (a) diagonal squares, *(b) vertical columns, (c) horizontal rows, (d) all adjacent squares.

2. Isotopes (a) have the same Z and N numbers, (b) are located in vertical columns, (c) have the same Z and N numbers but different radioactive properties, *(d) have the same Z but different N numbers.

3. Long-lived radioactive nuclides found in nature are indicated on the chart by a (a) white square, (b) gray square, *(c) black-topped square, (d) vertically divided square.

4. An isobaric series on the chart *(a) runs diagonally from lower right to upper left, (b) is a decay series, (c) is composed of a family of isotopes, (d) is all adjacent nuclides.

5. Which one of the following has the same Z and N numbers? (a) isobars, (b) isotones, *(c) isomers, (d) isotopes.

Experiment 54   DETECTION OF NUCLEAR RADIATION:
                 THE GEIGER COUNTER

Comments and Hints

    A good introduction to and understanding of the Geiger
counter is important in doing experiments on nuclear half-
life and absorption which follow.   In this experiment,
the Geiger tube voltage, count rate, and inverse square
law are investigated.

Answers to Selected Experiment Questions

3.   Inverse square law is for a point source.

4. N_1 = 8000 cpm, r_1 = 5 cm, and r_2 = 20 cm.

      $$N_2 = (r_1/r_2)^2 N_1 = (5/20)^2(8000) = 500 \text{ cpm}$$

POST-LAB QUIZ QUESTIONS

Completion

1.   The gas in a Geiger tube is usually argon .

2.   The process of successive ionizations of secondary elec-
      trons in a Geiger tube is called cumulative ionization .

3.   The current pulse counted in a Geiger counter is the
      result of a(n) avalanche discharge.

4.   After a current pulse, the time the tube voltage is
      less than that required to detect other radiation
      is called the dead (recovery) time .

5.   The more sensitive type of Geiger tube has a(n) end
      window.

6.   The lowest applied voltage of a Geiger tube that will
      give a count is called the threshold (starting)
      voltage.

7.   The count rate is almost linearly proportional to
      the tube voltage between threshold and the plateau
      region.

8. A geiger tube acts as a proportional counter in the voltage range between __threshold__ and the __plateau__ region.

9. The count rate is almost independent of the tube voltage in the __plateau__ region.

10. The count rate falls off as the __inverse square__ of the distance from the source.

Multiple Choice

1. The potential difference between the central wire and the cylinder of a Geiger tube decreases during (a) cumulative ionization, *(b) avalanche discharge, (c) the voltage change from threshold to the plateau region, (d) the recovery time.

2. A geiger counter cannot count (a) during cumulative ionization, (b) in the plateau region, *(c) below threshold voltage, (d) after a dead time period.

3. If a Geiger tube is moved three times as close to a radioactive source, the count rate (a) decreases by a factor of 4, (b) decreases by a factor of 6, (c) increases by a factor of 4, *(d) increases by a factor of 9.

Experiment 55   RADIOACTIVE HALF-LIFE

Comments and Hints

The minigenerator and the short half-life of the Ba-137m isomer allows the determination of a radioactive half-life in a relatively short time. However, because of the liquid sample, proper caution should be exercised so as not to have students radioactively "contaminated".

There is not a great deal of danger with a drop or two from the "cow" and the short Ba-137m half-life, but it should be emphasized to the students that they are working with radioactive material that could be spilled and cause contamination. You might ask your students if there should be proper shielding and have them justify their answers.

Answers to Selected Experiment Questions

2. Reducing 12,000 cpm by half (-lives), the count rate goes to 6,000 cpm, 3,000 cpm, 1500 cpm, 750 cpm in 4 half-lives, so

$$t = nt_{\frac{1}{2}} = (4)(5.27 \text{ y}) = 21.1 \text{ y}$$

3. Cs-137 has a half-life of $t_{\frac{1}{2}} = 30$ years, and $t_{\frac{1}{2}} = 0.693\tau$,

so $\tau = t_{\frac{1}{2}}/0.693 = 30/0.693 = 43$ years, and $N/N_o = e^{-t/\tau} = e^{-t/43}$.

(a) With $t = 5$ y,
$$N/N_o = e^{-t/43} = e^{-5/43} = e^{-0.12} = 0.89$$

and $N = 0.89N_o$. Taking N in terms of μCi, with $N_o = 10\mu$Ci,

$N = 0.89N_o = 0.89(10) = 8.9$ μCi.

(b) Activity = 8.9 μCi (3.7 x 10^4 dis/s/1 μCi)

= 3.3 x 10^5 dis (counts)/s

(c) Activity - 3.3 x 10^5 Bq

POST-LAB QUIZ QUESTIONS

Completion

1.   The decrease in the activity of a radioactive isotope is characterized by its half-life (or time constant) .

2.   The time constant of a radioactive decay is less than (0.693) its half-life .

3.   In 3 half-lives, the activity of a sample decreases by 7/8 .

4.   Nuclear activity is commonly expressed in counts per time (cpm) or Ci .

5.   The isotope used for half-life determination in the experiment is Ba-137m .

6.   BA-137m decays by gamma decay into Ba-137 .

7.   The parent nucleus in the beta decay process to Ba-137m is Cs-137 .

8.   In terms of count rate, 1 Bq is equal to 1 cps .

Multiple Choice

1.   The time constant of a radioactive decay process (a) has units of inverse time, (b) may be negative, (c) is expressed in cpm, *(d) is always less than the half-life of the process.

2.   For the activity of a radioactive sample to decrease below 10 percent of its original activity requires how many complete half-lives? (a) 2, *(b) 3, (c) 4, (d) 5

3.   Ba-137m is an isomeric state of *(a) Ba-137, (b) Cs-137 (c) hydrochloric acid, (d) Cs-137m.

Exp. 55

Essay

1. Discuss how radioactive isotopes may be used in radioactive dating where the original activity and half-
life of an isotope are known. (Radioactive dating
is used to determine how old an object is by observing
the present activity of a unit mass of a radioactive
isotope.)

Experiment 56   THE ABSORPTION OF NUCLEAR RADIATIONS

Comments and Hints

The absorption of nuclear radiations is important in many applications. The experiment gives students an appreciation of the range of nuclear radiations. They are often surprised at the results which gives an insight to nuclear shielding.

Answers to Selected Experiment Questions

2. $\mu_m = 0.1$ cm^2/g, x = 0.25 cm, $\rho_{Pb} = 11.3$ g/cm^3

   $\mu = \mu_m = (11.3)(0.1) = 1.13$ cm^{-1}

   $I/I_o = e^{-\mu x} = e^{-(1.13)(0.25)} = e^{-0.28} = 0.76$

Hence, 24% is absorbed.

4. $\mu_m = 0.058$ cm^2/g, x = 3 cm, $\rho_{Fe} = 7.86$ g/cm^3

   $\mu = \mu_m = (7.86)(0.058) = 0.46$ cm^{-1}

   $I/I_o = e^{-\mu x} = e^{-(0.46)(3)} = e^{-1.38} = 0.25$ or 25%

POST-LAB QUIZ QUESTIONS

Completion

1.   The absorption or degree of penetration of particle radiation depends on the electric charge and speed of the particles.

2.   Electrically charged radiations generally have shorter penetration distances.

3.   LET stands for linear energy transfer .

4. The linear absorption coefficient has units of cm^{-1} .

5. Gamma rays absorption varies exponentially in a material.

6. Unlike beta rays, gamma rays have no definite stopping range .

7. In a half-thickness, the radiation intensity is reduced by one-half (50%) .

8. The half-thickness of a material is inversely proportional to the linear absorption coefficient .

9. For a particular material, the linear absorption coefficient varies from sample to sample, but the mass absorption coefficient is the same.

10. Cs-137 is a beta-gamma radiation source.

Multiple Choice

1. In general, the least penetrating type of radiation is *(a) alpha, (b) beta, (c) gamma, (d) neutrons

2. The greater the charge and the slower a particle, the greater its (a) penetration, (b) range, *(c) LET, (d) linear absorption coefficient.

3. The absorption of gamma radiation depends on the (a) definite stopping range, *(b) radiation energy, (c) beta radiation range, (d) mass of the gamma rays.

4. In 3 half-thicknesses, what fraction of the incident gamma ray intensity would be absorbed? (a) 1/8, (b) 1/2, (c) 1/4, *(d) 7/8.

Essay

1. Discuss some applications where the absorption of nuclear radiations is important.

Experiment 57 THE PI-MU-e DECAY PROCESS

Comments and Hints

It is rare that an elementary particle experiment can be done in an introductory physics lab. The analysis of hydrogen bubble chamber photographs gives students some insight into how elementary particles are detected and investigated.

Although acceptable track drawings are shown in the experiment, it is helpful to show students several acceptable tracks (along with an unacceptable track or two) on a bubble chamber photograph.

Answers to Selected Experiment Questions

1. The rest mass of the positron accounts for only a small part (about 0.5%) of the muon's rest mass and the neutrinos are massless, so the total energy of the positron is equal to its kinetic energy to a good approximation.

2. No, they are charged particles moving in a magnetic field. However, the muons travel only a short distance before coming to rest and the track appears essentially linear.

POST-LAB QUIZ QUESTIONS

Completion

1. The π^+ meson is called a _pion_ .

2. The μ^+ meson is called a _muon_ .

3. The positron is the _antiparticle_ of an electron.

4. Photographic records of elementary particles are a result of trails of _ionization_ .

5. Neutrinos from the muon decay leave no tracks because they are _uncharged_ and produce no _ionization_ .

6. The term $K + m_o c^2$ is the _total relativistic energy_ .

7. The term $m_o c^2$ is called the _rest mass_ .

8. The average momentum or average length of a track is obtained by dividing the average value of the _perpendicular_ component by the average value of $\sin\theta$ (e.g., $\overline{p \sin\theta} = \overline{p_\perp}$ $p = \overline{p_\perp / \sin\theta}$) .

9. The track length of a particle that is created and loses all of its energy inside the bubble chamber corresponds to the particle's _range_ in the liquid hydrogen.

10. On the average, each of the decay products in muon decay receives _one-third_ of the total muon energy.

Multiple Choice

1. The antiparticle of an electron is a (a) pion, (b) muon, *(c) positron, (d) neutrino.

2. Which one of the following particles leaves no track in a bubble chamber? (a) pion, (b) muon, (c) positron, *(d) neutrino

3. All of the product particles in the $\pi - \mu - e$ decay process are positively charged as a result of the conservation of (a) mass, *(b) charge, (c) momentum, (d) energy.

4. The total relativistic energy of a particle is equal to its kinetic energy plus

   (a) pc, *(b) $m_o c^2$, (c) $p \sin\theta$, (d) $2K(m_o c^2)$.

LABORATORY SAFETY REFERENCES

Laboratory safety is of prime importance. References for books and manuals on this topic are given below. It is recommended that one or more of these be kept in the laboratory and that students be encouraged (if not required) to read pertinent safety procedures on given experiments and procedures.

AAPT, <u>Teaching Physics Safely</u>, (Some Practical Guidelines in Seven Areas of Common Concern in Physics Classrooms), AAPT Committee on Apparatus, AAPT Publications Dept., Suite 101, 5110 Roanoke Place, College Park, MD, 20740.

Armitage, P. and Fasemore, J., <u>Laboratory Safety, A Science Teacher's Source Book</u>, Heinemann Educational Books, London, 1977.

Brown, B. and Brown, W., <u>Science Teaching and the Law</u>, National Science Teachers Association, Washington, DC, 1969.

Bullen, T., "Safety in the Physics Laboratory", <u>The Physics Teacher</u>, December, 1974, pp. 579-583.

Everett, K. and Jenkins, E., <u>A Safety Handbook For Science Teachers</u>, John Murray, London, 1973.

Steere, N., Editor, <u>CRC Handbook of Laboratory Safety</u>, 2nd ed., CRC Press, Chemical Rubber Co., 1971.

Virdeh, A., "Safety Precautions Recommended for University Laboratories", <u>J. of Environmental Health</u>, November/December, 1969, pp. 295-297.

Virkus, R., Editor, <u>Safety in the Secondary Science Classroom</u>, National Science Teachers Association, Washington, DC, 1978. (Prepared by the NSTA Subcommittee on Safety.)

SCIENTIFIC EQUIPMENT SUPPLIERS

There are a large number of scientific equipment suppliers, some more specialized than others. A list of suppliers of general equipment and supplies used in the physics laboratory is presented here for your convenience. Sources of specific items may be found by consulting their individual catalogs which are generally available on request.

- Bernard O. Beck & Co.

  P.O. Box 272
  Arlington, TX 76010

- Carolina Physical Science
  (Carolina Biological Supply Co.)

  2700 York Rd.   Box 187
  Burlington, NC 27215   Gladstone, OR 97027

  1-800-344-5551   1-800-547-1733
  (In NC) 1-800-632-1231   (In OR) (503) 656-1641
                                                  (collect)

- Central Scientific Co.

  11222 Melrose Ave.
  Franklin Park, IL 60131-1364

  (312) 451-0150

- Daedalon Corp.

  P.O. Box 2028
  35 Congress St.
  Salem, MA 01970

  (617) 744-5310

- The Ealing Corp.

  Pleasant St.
  South Natick, MA 01760

  (617) 655-7000

- Edmund Scientific

  101 E. Gloucester Pike
  Barrington, NJ   08007

  1-800-222-0224
  (In NJ) (609) 547-3488

- Fisher Scientific

  Educational Materials
  4901 West LeMoyne St.
  Chicago, IL   60651

  (312) 378-7770
  1-800-621-4769

- Frey Scientific Co.

  905 Hickory Lane
  Mansfield, OH   44905

  1-800-225-FREY
  (In OH) (419) 589-9905 (collect)

- Klinger Education Products Corp.

  83-45 Parsons Blvd.
  Jamaica, NY   11432

  (718) 297-8080
       657-0536

- Metrologic Instruments, Inc.

  143 Harding Ave.
  P.O. box 307
  Bellmawr, NJ   08031-0307

  (609) 933-0100

- Pasco Scientific   (In Canada) Merlan Scientific, Ltd

  1876 Sabre St.   247 Armstrong Ave.
  Hayward, CA   94545   Georgetown, Ontario
                                                   Canada   L7G 4X6
  (415) 786-2800
  1-800-772-8700   (416) 877-0171
  (In CA, AK, and HI, call collect)   846-0646

- Sargent-Welch

  7300 North Linder Ave.
  P.O. Box 1026
  Skokie, IL 60077

  (312) 677-0600

- Thornton Associates, Inc.

  87 Beaver St.
  Waltham, MA 02154

  (617) 899-1400

(In Canada)

285 Garyray Dr.
Weston, Ontario
Canada M9L 1P3

(416) 741-5210

115 New Montgomery St.
San Francisco, CA 94105

(415) 495-3880

Major Equipment Needs

As stated in the preface of the laboratory manual, "This manual was written with the small college and university in mind. Laboratory equipment at such institutions is often limited, and available equipment is usually of the standard variety purchased from scientific supply companies. The experimental procedures in this manual are described for different types of common laboratory apparatus, thus maximizing the application of the manual."

Not only is the application of the manual maximized, but also the use of equipment. All of us like to introduce new experiments in our physics labs to provide a greater application of physical principles in instruction and a greater selection in the experiments that may be done. This, of course, is usually expensive. However, some equipment can be used in more than one experiment. To show the major, relatively costly equipment needs for each experiment and to assist you in planning, the following summary is made. Like superscripts on the experiment numbers indicates that the same equipment is used in these experiments. Relatively inexpensive, but necessary items are listed in parentheses.

It is assumed that general items used in a variety of experiments, such as meter sticks, string, weights (masses), balances, timers, thermometers, etc., are already available in the lab. A complete list of equipment needed for each experiment is given in Section II of each experiment in the manual.

Major Equipment Needs

Experiment

1   Experimental Error and Data Analysis

                 NONE

2[a]   Mass, Volume, and Density

                 (Vernier caliper)   [a](micrometer caliper)

3   Measuring the Height of a building

                 NONE

4   The Scientific Method: The Simple Pendulum

                 NONE

5[b]   Uniformly Accelerated Motion

                 A.   NONE

                 B.   spark-timer apparatus

                 [b]C.   linear air track

6   The Addition and Resolution of Vectors:
         The Force Table

                 force table

7   Newton's Second Law: The Atwood Machine

                 (precision pulley)

Experiment

8[b]   Conservation of Linear Momentum: The Air Track

               [b]linear air track

9   Projectile Motion: The Ballistic Pendulum

               ballistic pendulum

10   Centripetal Force

               A. motorized centripetal force apparatus
               B. manual centripetal force apparatus

11   Friction

               NONE

12[c]   Work and Energy

               [c](inclined plane)

13   Torque, Equilibrium, and Center of Gravity

               NONE

14[c]   Simple Machines: Mechanical Advantage and
               Efficiency

               [c](inclined plane)

               (wheel and axle)

Experiment

22[d,e]   Specific Heat of Metals

              [d](steam generator

              [e](calorimeter)

23[d,e]   Heats of Fusion and Vaporization

              [d](steam generator)

              [e](calorimeter)

24   Newton's Law of Cooling: The Time Constant
              of a Thermometer

              (metal-stem dial thermometer)

25   Archimedes' Principle: Buoyancy and
              Specific Gravity

                   NONE

Note: in the following electrical experiments, there is
a wide variety of selection and price ranges on various items.
Consult suppliers' catalogs. Multiscale ammeters and volt-
meters may be used in several experiments. Appropriate power
supplies are assumed available and not listed.

26[f]   Fields and Equipotentials
              [f]galvanometer

27[g,h,i,j]   Ohm's Law

              [g]ammeter   [i]decade resistance box

              [h]voltmeter   [j]rheostat (low ohm)

Experiment

$28^{f,g,h,j}$ The Potentiometer: emf and Terminal Voltage

         slide-wire potentiometer   standard cell

         ^{f}galvanometer ^{h}voltmeter

         ^{g}ammeter ^{j}rheostat (low ohm)

$29^{f,i}$ The Ammeter and Voltmeter: Meter Sensitivity

         ^{f}galvanometer   rheostat (high ohm)

         ^{i}decade resistance box

$30^{f,g,h,i,j}$ The Measurement of Resistance

         A. ^{g}ammeter ^{j}rheostat (low ohm)

             ^{h}voltmeter

         B. ^{f}galvanometer ^{i}decade resistance box

$31^{a,g,h,i}$ Resistivity

         ^{g}ammeter ^{j}rheostat (low ohm)

         ^{h}voltmeter ^{a}(micrometer caliper)

32^{i} The Temperature Dependence of Resistance

         slide-wire Wheatstone bridge

         ^{i}decade resistance box

$33^{g,h}$ Resistances in Series and Parallel

         ^{g}ammeter ^{h}voltmeter

Experiment

34[g,h]   Multiloop Circuits: Kirchhoff's Rules

                    [g]ammeter   [h]voltmeter

35[i,g,h]   Joule Heat

                    electrocaloimeter   [g]ammeter

                    [i]rheostat (low ohm)   [h]voltmeter

36[i,k]   The Measurement of Capacitance: Bridge Method

                    standard capacitor
                    [i]two decade resistance boxes

                    [k]audio-signal generator

                    telephone receiver

37   The RC Time Constant

                    infinite resistance (electrostatic) voltmeter

                    or vacuum tube voltmeter (VTVM)

38[k,l]   Introduction to the Oscilloscope

                    [k]audio-signal generator

                    [l]oscilloscope

39[k,l]   The RC Circuit: Oscilloscope Study

                    [k]audio-signal generator

                    [l]oscilloscope

Experiment

40[k,l]   Phase Measurements and Resonance in ac Circuits

                [k]audio-signal generator

                [l]oscilloscope

                decade resistance box (high ohm)

                air core inductor

41[f]   Electrostatic Induction

                pair of cylindrical coils with metal cores

                [f]galvanometer

42[k,l]   Rectification: Semiconductor Diodes

                [k]audio-signal generator

                [l]oscilloscope

43[h,k,l]   Transistor Characteristics

                millammeter (dc) Optional: [k]audio-signal
                                                generator
                microammeter (dc)
                                            [l]oscilloscope
                [h]voltmeter   earphones
                                                (high ohm)

44   Reflection and Refraction

                NONE

45   Spherical Mirrors and Lenses

                NONE

153

Experiment

46   Optical Instruments: The Microscope and
            Telescope

                    NONE

47   Polarized Light

                    Optional: exposure meter

48[m]   The Prism Spectrometer: Dispersion and Index
            of Refraction

                    [m]spectrometer

49[m,n]   Line Spectra and the Rydberg Constant

                    [m]spectrometer
                    [n]discharge tube (Hg or He, and H)
                        and power supply

50[m,n]   The Transmission Diffraction Grating:
            Measuring the Wavelength of Light

                    [m]spectrometer
                    [n]discharge tube (Hg) and power supply

51[j,g]   The Mass of an Electron: e/m Measurement

                    tuning-eye vacuum tube   [j]rheostat (low ohm)
                    air core solenoid   [g]ammeter
                    ac power supply

154

Experiment

52   Exponential Functions

                    NONE

53   The Chart of Nuclides

                    NONE

54^{o,p} Detection of Radiation: The Geiger Counter

                    ^{o}Geiger counter
                    ^{p}(radioactive source)

55° Radioactive Half-life

                    ^{o}Geiger counter
                         (Cs-137/Ba-137m minigenerator)

56^{o,p} The Absorption of Nuclear Radiations

                    ^{o}Geiger counter
                    ^{p}(radioactive source)

57   The Pi-Mu-e Decay Process

                    NONE

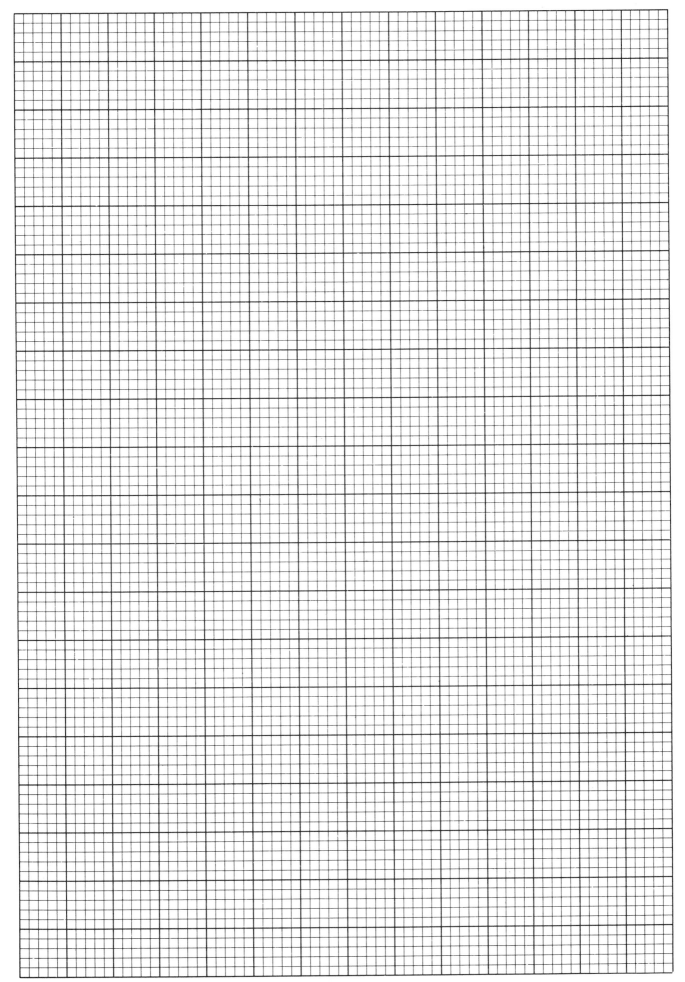

10 DIVISIONS PER INCH

10 DIVISIONS PER CENTIMETER

10
9
8
7
6
5
4
3
2
1

SEMI-LOGARITHMIC 1 CYCLE BY 10 DIVISIONS PER INCH

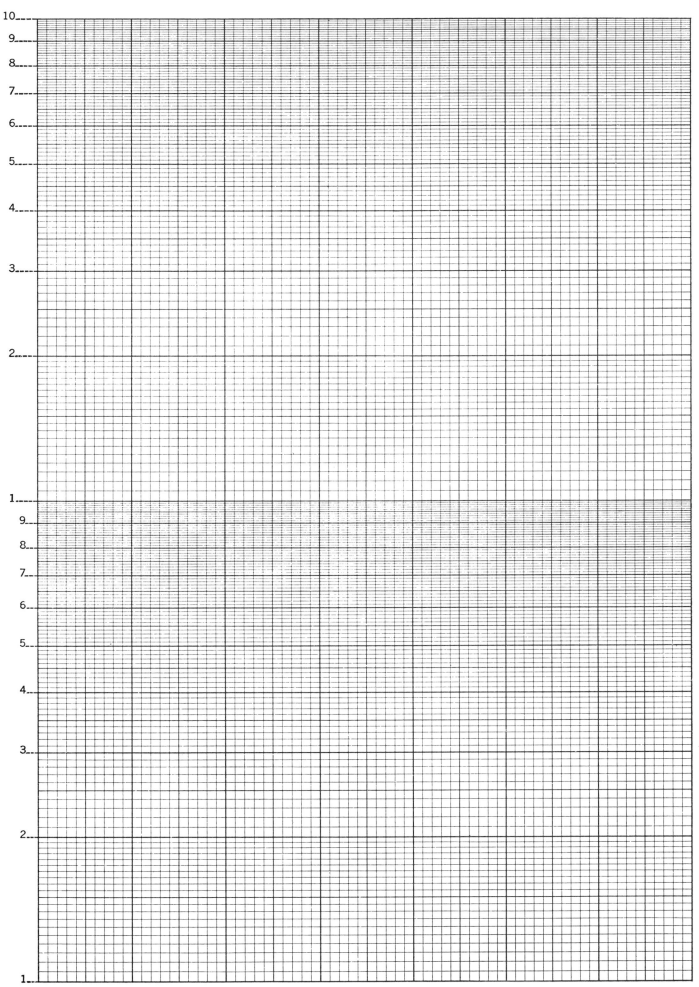

SEMI-LOGARITHMIC 2 CYCLES BY 10 DIVISIONS PER INCH

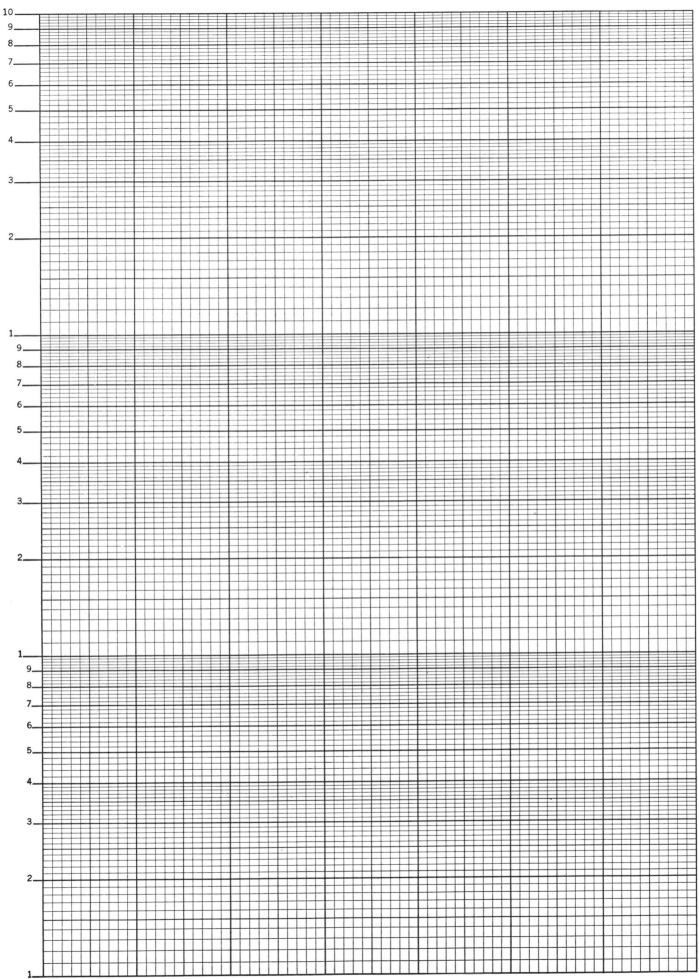

SEMI-LOGARITHMIC 3 CYCLES BY 10 DIVISIONS PER INCH

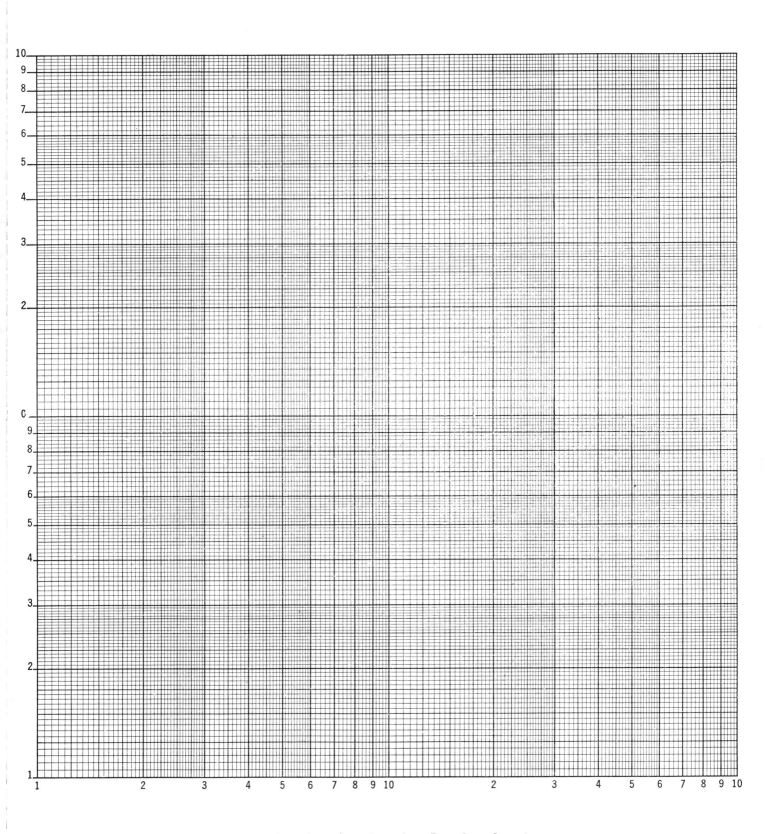

LOGARITHMIC 2 CYCLES BY 2 CYCLES